W9-BOK-765

Please remember that this is a library book,
and that it belongs only temporarily to each
person who uses it. Be considerate. Do
not write in this, or any, library book.

WITHDRAWN

THE MEDIEVAL LIBRARY UNDER
THE GENERAL EDITORSHIP OF
SIR ISRAEL GOLLANCZ, Litt.D., F.B.A.

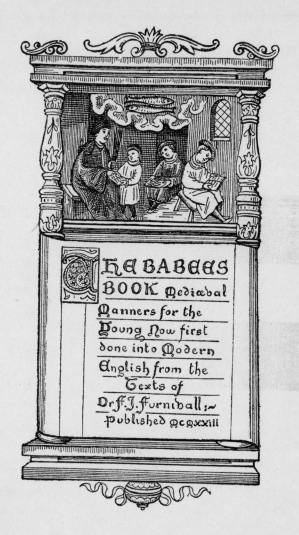

The engraved title on the reverse of this page was adapted by Miss Blanche C. Hunter from B.M. Add. MS. 31240, f. 4.

The School of Aristotle.
see page 9.

THE BABEES' BOOK:
MEDIEVAL MANNERS FOR THE YOUNG : DONE INTO MODERN ENGLISH FROM DR. FURNIVALL'S TEXTS BY EDITH RICKERT

COOPER SQUARE PUBLISHERS, INC.
NEW YORK
1966

Published 1966 by Cooper Square Publishers, Inc.
59 Fourth Avenue, New York, N. Y. 10003
Library of Congress Catalog Card No. 66-30205

Printed in the United States of America
by Noble Offset Printers, Inc., New York, N. Y. 10003

395
F989b

CONTENTS

19763

ILLUSTRATIONS

INTRODUCTION

NEARLY forty years ago, Dr. Furnivall collected for the Early English Text Society " divers treatises touching the Manners and Meals of Englishmen in former days." Some of these were published in 1868, under the title *The Babees' Book*,[1] and others, chiefly of later date, in 1869, under the title *Queene Elizabethes Achademy*.

These two volumes, with their introductions and illustrative matter, to my mind present the most vivid picture of home life in medieval England that we have. Aside from their general human interest, they are valuable to the student of social history, and almost essential to an understanding of the literature of their time. The whole fabric of the romances was based upon the intricate system of " courtesy " as here set forth, and John Russell furnishes an interesting com-

---

[1] Since listed as *Early English Meals and Manners*.

ment on Chaucer and his school, as do Rhodes and
Seager and Weste on the writers of the sixteenth
century.   Finally, among these treatises, there is many
a plum by the way for the seeker of proverbs, curious
lore, superstitions, literary oddities.   And as compara-
tively few people have time or inclination to worry
through antiquated English, Dr. Furnivall has long
wished that the substance of his collections might
be presented in modern form.   Therefore this little
volume has been undertaken.

Doubtless unwritten codes of behaviour are coeval
with society; but the earliest treatises that we possess
emphasize morals rather than manners.   Even the late
Latin author known as Dionysius Cato (fourth century ?), whose maxims were constantly quoted, translated, imitated, and finally printed during the late
Middle Ages, does not touch upon the niceties of conduct that we call manners ; wherefore one John Garland, an Englishman educated at Oxford, who lived
much in France during the first half of the thirteenth
century, felt bound to supplement Cato on these
points.   His work, entitled *Liber Faceti : docens mores
hominum, precipue iuuenum, in supplementum illorum qui*

a moralissimo Cathone erant omissi iuuenibus utiles,[1] is
alluded to as *Facet* in the first piece in this volume,
and serves as basis for part of the *Book of Courtesy*.

But, earlier than this, Thomasin of Zerklaere, about
1215, wrote in German a detailed treatise on manners
called *Der Wälsche Gast*.[2] And in 1265, Dante's
teacher, Brunetto Latini, published his *Tesoretto*,[2]
which was soon followed by a number of similar
treatises in Italian.

While we need not hold with the writer of the *Little
Children's Little Book*, that courtesy came down from
heaven when Gabriel greeted the Virgin, and Mary
and Elizabeth met, we must look for its origin some-
where ; and inasmuch as, in its medieval form at least,
it is closely associated with the practices of chivalry, we
may not unreasonably suppose it to have appeared first
in France.   And although most of the extant French
treatises belong to the fourteenth or fifteenth centuries,
a lost book of courtesy, translated by Thomasin of

[1] "The Book of the Polite Man, teaching manners for
men, especially for boys, as a supplement to those which
were omitted by the most moral Cato."

[2] Described and in part translated in an appendix to
Queene Elizabethes Achademy.

Zerklaere, is sometimes held, on good grounds, to have been derived from French, rather than from Italian.

In any case, such of the English books as were not taken immediately from Latin, came from French sources. To be sure, there is a Saxon poem, based it would seem on Cato, though by no means a translation, called *A Father's Instructions to his Son ;* but this, although it is greatly exercised about the child's soul, takes no thought for his finger-nails or his nose.

It is not, therefore, surprising to find that nearly all English words denoting manners are of French origin—*courtesy, villainy, nurture, dignity, etiquette, debonaire, gracious, polite, gentilesse, &c.*, while to balance them I can, at this moment, recall only three of Saxon origin—*thew* (which belongs rather to the list of moral words in which Old English abounds), *churlish* and *wanton* (without breeding), both of which, significantly enough, are negative of good manners.

The reason for the predominance of the French terms is simply that " French use these gentlemen," as one old writer puts it ; that is, from the Conquest until the latter part of the fourteenth century the language of the invaders prevailed almost entirely among the upper classes, who, accordingly, learned their politeness out of French or Latin books ; and it was only with the growth of citizenship and English together, that these matters came to be discussed in this latter tongue for the profit of middle-class children, as well as of the " bele babees " at Court.

We must suppose, from numerous hints and descriptions, that an elaborate system of manners and customs prevailed long before it was codified. The Bayeux tapestry (eleventh century) shows a feast, with a server kneeling to serve, his napkin about his neck, as John Russell prescribes some four hundred years later.

The romances again, alike in French and in English, describe elaborate ceremonies, and allude constantly to definite laws of courtesy. Now and again we find a passage that sets forth the ideal gentleman. Young Horn, for example, was taught " skill of wood and river " (hunting and hawking), carving, cup-bearing, and harping "with his nails sharp." Child Florent showed his high birth by his love of horse, hawk, and armour, and by his contempt of gold ; but he was not thought ill-mannered to laugh when his foster-father and mother fell down in their attempt to draw a rusty sword from its scabbard! Chaucer's *Squire* might well have been brought up on a treatise similar to those included in this volume :

> " Well could he sit on horse and fairly ride ;
>> He could songs make and fair could he indite,
>> Joust and eke dance, and well portray and write.
>
> .   .   .   .   .   .
>
>> Courteous he was, lowly, and serviceáble,
>> And carved before his father at the table."

But the *Prioress* outmatched him, having possibly learned her manners in the French of " Stratford-atte-Bowe," in *Les Contenances de la Table*, or some such thing :

> " At meatë well y-taught was she withal,
>> She let no morsel from her lippës fall,
>> Nor wet her fingers in her saucë deep :
>> Well could she carry a morsel, and well keep,
>> That no dropë did fall upon her breast ;
>> In courtesy was set full much her lest.[1]
>> Her over-lippë wipéd she so clean,
>> That in her cup there was no farthing seen
>> Of grease, when she drunken had her draught.

[1] Lust, *i.e.*, pleasure.

Full seemëly after her meat she raught,[1]
And certainly she was of great desport,[2]
And full pleasant, and amiable of port ;
And painéd her to counterfeitē cheer
Of court, and to be stately in mannér,
And to be holden digne of reverence."

These maxims were versified that they might be the
more easily remembered, as we know from various ex-
pressions, notably " Learn or be Lewd " (ignorant),
which occurs at the end of several pieces. In 1612 the
principle was stated explicitly, " because children will
learn that book with most readiness and delight through
the running of the metre, as it is found by experience."
And the fact that versified treatises on manners formed
part of the schooling of that day, brings up the subject
of medieval education.

In the first place, this cannot be understood until we
have set aside our modern ideas of master and servant.
The old point of view is picturesquely summed up in a
pamphlet of 1598, quoted by Dr. Furnivall.

" Amongst what sort of people should then this

[1] Reached.   [2] Mirth.

serving-man be sought for ?   Even the duke's son
preferred page to the prince, the earl's second son
attendant upon the duke, the knight's second son the
earl's servant, the esquire's son to wear the knight's
livery, and the gentleman's son the esquire's serving-
man. Yea, I know at this day gentlemen, younger
brothers that wear their elder brother's blue coat and
badge, attending him with as reverent regard and duti-
ful obedience as if he were their prince or sovereign.
Where was then in the prime of this profession Good-
man Tomson's Jack, or Robin Rush, my Gaffer Russet-
coat's second son ? The one holding the plough, the
other whipping the cart-horse, labouring like honest
men in their vocation. Trick Tom the tailer was then
a tiler for this trade ; as strange to find a blue coat on
his back, with a badge on his sleeve, as to take Kent
Street without a scold, or Newmarket Heath without
a highwayman. But now, being lapped in his livery,
he thinketh himself as good a man, with the shears at
his back, as the Poet Laureate with a pen in his ear."

From this passage it is clear that at a time not very
much earlier, serving was a profession in which every
rank, except royalty itself (if indeed this is to be

omitted, see pp. 1, 179 below), might honourably wear the livery of a man of higher rank.   Indeed, under the system of entail, this was, in time of peace, the only possible livelihood for a gentleman's younger son, unless he had a special aptitude for law or the Church. Debarred from all trade, he could only offer his services to some great man who was compelled by his estate to keep up a large household, and so earn his patronage to provide for the future.   It was fully expected that boys so placed would be helped to opportunities at Court or abroad, and girls to good marriages.   That these patrons really took an interest in their young servitors, and felt responsible for their welfare, appears in many accounts of help bestowed upon men who afterwards became famous in literature, or scholarship, or statecraft.   And as for the girls, Dr. Furnivall quotes an amusing instance of a mistress who, when reproached with dismissing a gentlewoman without due cause, thereby injuring her chances for the future, immediately allowed her forty shillings a year towards her maintenance while she herself lived.

Among rich men it was the custom to receive a number of boys for training in this way.   In the house-

hold of Lord Percy there were nine young " henchmen " who served him as cup-bearers and in various
other capacities. To these he allowed servants, one
for each two, unless they were " at their friends' finding," in which case they might have one apiece.
Likewise, in his household, his second son was carver,
his third, sewer.

But while in a rich man's household, younger sons
might receive as good a training as if they had been sent
elsewhere for the purpose, the case of the younger sons
of a poor gentleman might be sufficiently wretched.
Orlando, in *As You Like It*, speaks feelingly on this
point. Although his father had left 1000 crowns for
his upbringing, he was so neglected that he says : " His
(his brother's) horses are bred better, for, besides that
they are fair with their feeding, they are taught their
manage, and to that end riders dearly hired ; [1] but I,
his brother, gain nothing under him but growth . . .
he lets me feed with his hinds, bars me the place of a

[1] So Ascham: "It is pity, that commonly more care
is had, yea, and that among very wise men, to find out
rather a cunning man for their horse than a cunning man
for their children."

brother, and as much as in him lies, mines my gentility with my education."

The alternative to such a life of hardship was either to enter the Church or depend upon its charity, or to serve in the household of a man of rank.   While only a few were fitted for the religious life or cared to undertake it, " many poor gentlemen . . . left beggars in consequence of the inheritance devolving to the eldest son," were supported by the charity of the Church, as we are told by an Italian visitor to England in 1496–7.

The case of an unmarried daughter living at home, though less desperate, was even in well-to-do families sufficiently uncomfortable, as is plainly hinted in a letter written by Margaret Paston to her husband in 1469.   She implores him to find his sister " some worshipful place," and concludes : " I will help to her finding, for we be either of us weary of other."

The practice of sending children seven or eight years old away from their parents was ostensibly that they " might learn better manners " ; but the Italian visitor mentioned above concluded uncharitably that the real reason was, the English had but small affection for their children, and liked to keep all their comforts

to themselves, and moreover knew that they would be
" better served by strangers than by their own children."   However absurd this may seem at first glance,
I incline to think that the foreigner may have touched
upon truth here, as is borne out by many instances of
Spartan, even brutal, treatment of children by parents
in those days.   Still, the fact remains that the loss of
home life and parental tenderness was balanced by
gain in discipline, education, social opportunity, and
the opening up of careers.

The education of the various children addressed in
these treatises varied according to their social status.
As early as the twelfth century certainly, and perhaps
earlier, it was customary for " bele babees," with boys
and girls, to have a tutor either at home, or in the household of the great man with whom they were placed.
If they went to school, there were at first the monastic
and conventual institutions ; then later, the universities and grammar-schools.   But, in the case of
girls like the *Good Wife's* daughter, who sold homespun in the market-place, and had to be admonished
not to get drunk often, I doubt whether there would
be any education beyond her mother's teaching.

The universities, at first, were frequented chiefly by

poor men's sons, and scarcely attended by the upper classes. In Chaucer's time, the *Clerk of Oxenford* was lean and threadbare, and had but little gold, and his two Cambridge scholars were in no better case. Nearly two centuries later, Sir Thomas More says : " Then may we yet like poor scholars of Oxford, go a-begging with our bags and wallets, and sing ' *Salve, Regina* ' " (a carol) " at rich men's doors." However, gradually during the sixteenth century, a university education became so fashionable that rich men's sons crowded in, and " scrooged " (I quote Dr. Furnivall) poor students out of the proceeds of endowments left expressly for them. Still, in 1517, the old ideal of a gentleman as yet held its own, as is amusingly related by Pace in his *De Fructu.* He tells how " one of those whom we call gentlemen, who always carry some horn hanging at their backs, as though they would hunt during dinner, said : ' I swear by God's body I would rather that my son should hang than study letters. For it becomes the sons of gentlemen to blow the horn nicely, and to hunt skilfully, and elegantly carry and train a hawk. But the study of letters should be left to the sons of rustics. . . .' "

But Pace was equal to him. " You do not seem to

me to think aright, good man," said I, "for if any
foreigner were to come to the king, such as are ambas-
sadors of princes, and an answer had to be given to him,
your son if he were educated as you wish, could only
blow his horn, and the learned sons of rustics would be
called to answer, and they would be far preferred to
your hunter or fowler son," &c.

The fashion among noblemen of sending their sons
abroad to study, either at a university or with a tutor,
did not prevail widely until later. In the twelfth
century, indeed, the "English nation" was famous at
the University of Paris, but was composed largely of
poor but earnest students, some of whom became
famous men ; and even these had ceased to study there
before the fifteenth century.

Younger sons of good birth, in the service of a man
of rank, were usually taught by a "maistyr" or tutor
in the household in which they were placed. It is only
in later books like Seager's that these rules of demeanour
were applied extensively to schoolboys. Doubtless
gentlemen's sons went to Winchester (after 1373) and
to Eton (after 1440) ; but of the thirty grammar-
schools endowed before 1500, all the others were

attended chiefly by the middle classes. The early monastic schools doubtless entertained young noblemen; but the cathedral schools founded by Henry VIII. seem to have been for citizens' children, such as the boy in Symon's *Lesson of Wisdom*, who is urged to learn fast so that when the old bishop dies he may be ready to take his place. However, even earlier we find complaints of the monastic schools which helped each shoemaker to educate his son, and each beggar's brat to be a writer and finally a bishop, so that lords' sons must kneel to him.

In general, the system of education implied in the *Babees' Book* is that described in the household ordinances of Edward IV. for the young henchmen in charge of a "maistyr," who should teach them to ride cleanly and surely, to draw them also to jousts, to . . . wear their harness, to have all courtesy in words, deeds, and degrees, diligently to keep them in rules of goings and sittings, after they be of honour." They learned also "sundry languages," and harping, piping, singing and dancing. Likewise, their master sat always with them at table in the hall, to see "how mannerly they eat and drink, and to their communication and other forms of court, after the book of *Urbanitie*[1]" Clearly it would seem that one of the very treatises in this collection was studied by these young pages of Edward IV.

What languages they learned and what else studied we are not told in detail ; but in Henry VIII.'s time, young Gregory Cromwell, son of the Earl of Essex, studied French, writing, fencing, " casting accounts," instrumental music, &c. He was also made to read English aloud for the pronunciation, and was taught the etymology of Latin and French words. His day was as follows : After Mass, he read first the Colloquium on *Pietas Puerilis* (*De Civilitate Morum Puerilium*) by Erasmus (written 1530), of which he had to practice the precepts. Now this is nothing more than a collection of maxims similar to the *Facet* mentioned in the *Babees' Book*, together with learned *Scholia* in Latin and Greek ; hence, he had the same kind of thing to learn—only more elaborate— as the boys mentioned a hundred years earlier studied in *Urbanitie*. Doubtless his master approved the beginning of Erasmus : " Est autem uel prima uirtutis ac honestatis pars, tenere præcepta de moribus." The

---

[1] See p. 11, below.

specific nature of these directions appears in the following :

" Cleanliness of teeth must be cared for, but to whiten them with powder does for girls. To rub the gum with salt or alum is injurious. . . . If anything sticks to the teeth, you must get it out, not with a knife, or with your nails after the manner of dogs and cats, or with your napkin, but with a toothpick, or quill or small bone taken from the tibias of cocks or hens. To wash the mouth in the morning with pure water is both mannerly and healthful ; to do it often is foolish." Indeed, Erasmus's treatise is only a superior book of courtesy.

His manners attended to, young Gregory wrote for one or two hours, read Fabyan's *Chronicle*, and gave the rest of the day to his lute and virginals. When he rode, his master used to tell him stories of the Greeks and Romans, which he had to repeat; and his recreations were hunting, hawking and shooting with the long bow.

A harsher system prevailed with Queen Elizabeth's wards, according to Sir Nicholas Bacon. They went to church at 6 o'clock, studied Latin until 11, dined from 11 to 12, had music from 12 to 2, French from 2 to 3, Latin and Greek from 3 to 5, then prayers, supper, and "honest pastimes" until 8, then music until 9, and so to bed.

The curricula in these various schools doubtless emphasized the usual Latin subjects (Greek was not taught in England before 1500) of the Middle Ages. Thus we find an account of the "disputations" in a London grammar-school, dating from 1174. But that athletic sports were popular even at that early time, appears from the same narrative, in which we read of football, sham fights, water-quintain, archery, running, leaping, wrestling, stone-casting, flinging bucklers, sliding and skating (on bones), besides the brutal sports of hog-, boar- and cock-fighting, bull- and bear-baiting.

At the other extreme we find the account of a school-day in 1612. Work begins at 6, and those who come first have the best places. At 9 o'clock, there is given 15 minutes for breakfast and recreation; then work continues until 11 or past (to balance the 15 minutes off). Dinner follows, and then work until 3 or 3.30, then 15 minutes off, and work until 5.30, when school closes with a piece of a chapter, two staves of a psalm and prayer by the master.

It is probable, however, that these two descriptions are but two sides of the same medal ; that Fitzstephen's holidays were balanced by work days as tedious as those described by Brinsley.[1]

A singular fact to be noted in the English courtesy books is the almost complete absence of allusions to women.   Barring the *Good Wife* and *Wise Man*, which are distinctly middle class in tone, we have practically nothing to represent the elaborate directions for conduct in some of the foreign treatises.   Yet it cannot be doubted that the English system of patronage led to social problems and rules for the demeanour of young men and women together, such as prevailed abroad. Undoubtedly, too, the association of a lord's pages and a lady's maidens must have furthered the arrangement of marriages, perhaps not always in the way desired. Take, for example, the case of Anne Boleyn.   After seven years' service with the royal ladies of France, she came home and was placed in the household of Queen Katharine.   Meanwhile, there was attendant upon

[1] *The Grammar Schoole.* 1612.

Cardinal Wolsey a certain young Lord Percy, who, whenever his master was with the king, would " resort for pastime into the queen's chamber, and there would fall in dalliance among the queen's maidens."   In the end, he and Mistress Anne were secretly troth-plight ; but Wolsey discovered the arrangement and sent the girl home, whereat she " smoked " (we say *fumed*) until she was recalled and heard of the great love the king bore her " in the bottom of his stomach " ; then she " began to look very hault and stout, having all manner of jewels or rich apparel that might be gotten for money."   And doubtless there are many other similar complications to be found among old records, and more have perished, or were never written down at all.

It is something of a shock to turn from the elaborate rules for carving and serving, as set forth by Russell and others, to the domestic records of the time. The mingled splendour and squalor of the Middle Ages almost passes belief. We read of priceless hangings and costumes that cost each a small fortune, yet Erasmus describes the floors in noblemen's houses as sometimes encumbered with refuse for twenty years

together,[1]   King Edward IV. was provided with a
barber who shaved him once a week, and washed his
head, feet, and legs, *if* he so desired.   A proper bath,
according to Russell, seems to have been an event to
be heralded with flowers and resorted to chiefly as
curative.   We see to-day the splendid palaces and
castles, such as Hampton Court and Windsor, Knole
and Penshurst and Warwick, built by kings and
noblemen, and yet Henry VIII. had to enact a law
against the filthy condition of the servants in his own
kitchen, and Wolsey, passing through the suitors in
Westminster Hall, carried disinfectants concealed in
an orange.   It is this contrast in manners, doubtless,
which will first strike the reader.   A young nobleman
had to be instructed not only how to hold his carving-
knife with a thumb and two fingers, but also not to
dip his meat into the salt-cellar, or lick the dust out of
dish with his tongue, or wipe his nose on the table-
cloth ; and other instructions were added too primitive
for translation.   Undoubtedly, the general impres-

[1] But Erasmus was a Dutchman. Oddly enough, about
a century later, Pepys alludes to " these dirty Dutch
fellows."

sion that one derives is, as Dr. Furnivall puts it, of "dirty, ill-mannered, awkward young gawks," whose "maistyrs" were greatly to be pitied. But, on the whole, it is surprising to note how little the fundamental bases of good manners have altered. Though we are not to-day so plain-spoken, our ideals are similar to those of our ancestors, but theirs was the greater difficulty of attainment. Personal cleanliness, self-respect, reverence to one's better, and consideration for one's neighbour seem to have been then as they are now, the foundation-stones.

On the other hand, it is interesting to notice the development of manners with improved conditions of life. One code was altered with the introduction of the handkerchief, another with the use of the fork (apparently first mentioned in 1463, but not common until after 1600, though it had long been in use on the Continent), and so on, so that by degrees social expedients and ceremonies change, while essentials remain.

Of each of the pieces here included I give a brief account in the notes. Needless to say, they form only a small portion of an enormous practical literature, though they are fairly representative of the English

branch of it, for the time that they cover.   In order to
bring even so much within the compass of this small
volume, it has been found necessary to condense.   The
principle of condensation has been as follows : whenever a text is particularly wordy for the matter that it
contains, or has been found difficult to reproduce in
modern language in the old verse-form, it has been
done simply into prose.   In cases where the metrical
form has been preserved, perhaps both rhythm and
rhyme have suffered in the translation ; but in no
instance has there been any poetic beauty lost, for the
plain reason that the literary value of these produc-
tions is nil.   In addition to a few omissions on grounds
of taste, I have put aside various recipes and dietaries,
hoping to use them later in a book devoted entirely to
that sort of thing ; and for the same reason, I have
omitted considerable portions of Russell's work, in
which he deals with the dietetic properties and values
of different kinds of food, describes various sorts of
wines, enters into the details of carving fish, flesh, and
fowl, and sets forth numerous recipes and elaborate
menus.   It is all interesting but has little to do
with manners.   Likewise, I have omitted Wynkyn de

Worde's *Book of Carving*, which seems to be only a prose version of Russell, portions of Rhodes's work which deal rather with professional serving-men, and of Seager's and West's books, which treat of morals rather than manners. Further, I have omitted the various Latin and French poems on the subject, and a number of odds and ends of a generally didactic character, which, it seemed, could be best spared.

In translating, I have tried to keep as much as possible the quaint flavour of the originals, especially in the case of those rendered into modern English in the verse form. To that end I have retained old words and constructions whenever they seemed intelligible, although eccentric and perhaps ungrammatical to-day. When an archaic word alone conveyed the exact meaning, or was especially picturesque, I have left it, with a gloss at the bottom of the page, where also I refer to notes at the end, on points which seem to require special elucidation. My aim throughout has been to make the texts clear with the minimum of alteration. Doubtless I could have improved the metre frequently by merely a change in order of words ; but I thought it better to meddle as little as possible, except for the sake of clearness ; and so the verse often bumps along cheerfully, regardless of rhythm, style, and grammar. I think I may claim that in substance the modernised *Babees' Book* is as near as possible to its original.

About half of the translations have been made by Miss L. J. Naylor.

THE BABEES' BOOK

OR

A LITTLE REPORT OF HOW YOUNG PEOPLE SHOULD BEHAVE

MAY He who formed mankind in His image,
support me while I turn this treatise out of
Latin into my common language, that through this
little comment all of tender years may receive instruc-
tion in courtesy and virtue.

Facet [1] saith that the Book of Courtesy to teach the
practice of virtue is the most helpful thing in the world,
so I will not shrink from this labour or refuse it; but
for mine own learning will say something that touches
upon the matter.

But oh, young babies, whom blood royal hath endowed with grace, comeliness, and high ability, it is on
you I call to know this book, for it were great pity but

[1] *Liber Faceti.* See note.

that ye added to sovereign beauty virtue and good
manners.   Therefore I speak to you specially, and not
to old men expert in governance, decorum, and honest
manners, for what need is to give pangs to Hell, joy
to Heaven, water to the sea, or heat to fire already hot ?

And so, young babies,[1] my book is only for your in-
struction ; wherefore I pray that no man reprehend it,
but amend it where it is at fault, and judge it not, for
your own sake.   I seek no other reward but that it may
please men and give you some ease in learning.[1]   Also,
sweet children, if there be in it any word that ye ken
not, speer [2] while ye may, and when ye know it, bear
it in mind ; and so by asking you may learn of wise
men.   Also, think not too strangely that my pen
writes in this metre ; [1] for such verse is commonly
used, therefore take heed.

And first of all, I think to show how you babies who
dwell in households, should 'have [3] yourselves when ye
be set at meat, and how when men bid you be merry,
you should be ready with lovely, sweet and benign
words.   In this, aid me, O Mary, Mother Revered ;
and eke, O lady mine, Facetia,[1] guide thou my pen

---

[1] See note.   [2] Ask. Still used in Scotland.   [3] Behave.

and show unto me help. For as A is the first of all letters, so art thou mother of all virtue. Have pity, sweet lady, of my lack of wit, and though untaught I speak of demeanour, support my ignorance with thy goodly aid.

Ah, " bele [1] babees," hearken now to my lore.

When you enter your lord's place, say " God speed," and with humble cheer greet all who are there present. Do not rush in rudely, but enter with head up and at an easy pace, and kneel on one knee only to your lord or sovereign, whichever he be.

If any speak to you at your coming, look straight at them with a steady eye, and give good ear to their words while they be speaking ; and see to it with all your might that ye jangle [2] not, nor let your eyes wander about the house, but pay heed to what is said, with blithe visage and diligent spirit. When ye answer, ye shall be ready with what ye shall say, and speak " things fructuous," [3] and give your reasons smoothly, in words that are gentle but compendious,[4] for many

---

[1] See note. [2] Chatter.
[3] Fruitful, *i.e.*, useful. [4] Brief and to the point.

words are right tedious to the wise man who listens;
therefore eschew them with diligence.

Take no seat, but be ready to stand until you are
bidden to sit down. Keep your hands and feet at
rest; do not claw your flesh or lean against a post,
in the presence of your lord, or handle anything be-
longing to the house.

Make obeisance to your lord always when you answer;
otherwise, stand as still as a stone, unless he speak.

Look with one accord that if ye see any person better
than yourself come in, ye go backwards anon and give
him place, and in nowise turn your face from him, as
far forth as you may.

If you see your lord drinking, keep silence, without
loud laughter, chattering, whispering, joking or other
insolence.

If he command you to sit in his presence, fulfil his
wish at once, and strive not with another about your
seat.

When you are set down, tell no dishonest tale; eschew also, with all your might, to be scornful; and let
your cheer be humble, blithe, and merry, not chiding
as if ye were ready for a fight.

If you perceive that your better is pleased to commend you, rise up anon and thank him heartily.

If you see your lord and lady speaking of household matters, leave them alone, for that is courtesy, and interfere not with their doing; but be ready, without feigning, to do your lord service, and so shall you get a good name.

Also, to fetch him drink, to hold the light when it is time, and to do whatsoever ought to be done, look ye be ready; for so shall ye full soon get a gentle name in nurture. And if you should ask a boon of God, you can desire no better thing than to be well-mannered.

If your lord is pleased to offer you his own cup to drink, rise when you take it, and receive it goodly with both your hands, and when you have done, proffer it to no man else, but render it again to him that brought it, for in nowise should it be used commonly—so wise men teach us.

Now must I tell you shortly what you shall do at noon when your lord goes to his meat. Be ready to fetch him clear water, and some of you hold the towel for him until he has done, and leave not until he be set down, and ye have heard grace said. Stand before him until he bids you sit, and be always ready to serve him with clean hands.

When ye be set, keep your own knife clean and sharp, that so ye may carve honestly[1] your own meat.

Let courtesy and silence dwell with you, and tell no foul tales to another.

Cut your bread with your knife and break it not. Lay a clean trencher[2] before you, and when your pottage is brought, take your spoon and eat quietly; and do not leave your spoon in the dish, I pray you.

Look ye be not caught leaning on the table, and keep clear of soiling the cloth.

Do not hang your head over your dish, or in any wise drink with full mouth.

Keep from picking your nose, your teeth, your nails at meal-time—so we are taught.

Advise you against taking so muckle meat into your mouth but that ye may right well answer when men speak to you.

When ye shall drink, wipe your mouth clean with a

[1] Decorously. [2] See note.

cloth, and your hands also, so that you shall not in any way soil the cup, for then shall none of your companions be loth to drink with you.

Likewise, do not touch the salt in the salt-cellar with any meat ; but lay salt honestly on your trencher, for that is courtesy.

Do not carry your knife to your mouth with food, or hold the meat with your hands in any wise ; and also if divers good meats are brought to you, look that with all courtesy ye assay of each ; and if your dish be taken away with its meat and another brought, courtesy demands that ye shall let it go and not ask for it back again.

And if strangers be set at table with you, and savoury meat be brought or sent to you, make them good cheer with part of it, for certainly it is not polite when others be present at meat with you, to keep all that is brought you, and like churls vouchsafe nothing to others.

Do not cut your meat like field-men who have such an appetite that they reck not in what wise, where or when or how ungoodly they hack at their meat ; but, sweet children, have always your delight in courtesy

and in gentleness, and eschew boisterousness with all
your might.

When cheese is brought, have a clean trencher, on
which with a clean knife ye may cut it ; and in your
feeding look ye appear goodly, and keep your tongue
from jangling, for so indeed shall ye deserve a name
for gentleness and good governance, and always advance yourself in virtue.

When the end of the meal is come, clean your knives,
and look you put them up where they ought to be,[1] and
keep your seat until you have washed, for so wills
honesty.

When ye have done, look then that ye rise up without laughter or joking or boisterous word, and go to
your lord's table, and there stand, and pass not from
him until grace be said and brought to an end.

Then some of you should go for water, some hold
the cloth, some pour upon his hands.

Other things I might commend you to do, but as
my time is brief, I put them not into this little report ;
but overpass them, praying with a spirit that rejoices
in this labour, that no man abuse me ; but where too

[1] See note.

little is, let him add more, and where too much, let him take away, for though I would, time forbids that I say more. Therefore I take my leave, and inscribe this book to every wight whom it may please to correct it.

And, sweet children, for love of whom I write, I beseech you, with very loving heart, that you set your delight upon knowing this book; and may Almighty God that suffered bitter pains, make you so expert in courtesy that through your nurture and your governance you may advance yourselves to lasting bliss.

THE A B C OF ARISTOTLE

WHOSO wills to be wise and worship desires,
  Learn he one letter and look on another,
Of the A B C of Aristotle. Argue not against that.
It is counsel for right many clerks and knights a thousand,
And eke it might amend a man, full oft,
For to learn lore of one letter, and his life save;
For too much of any thing was never wholesome.
Read oft on this roll, and rule thee thereafter.
Whoso be grieved in his ghost, govern him better;
Blame he not the bairn that this A B C made,

But wite [1] he his wicked will and his work after.

It shall never grieve a good man, though the guilty be
    mended,

Now hearken and hear how I begin.

  Be not—

A too Amorous, too Adventurous, nor Argue too much.

B too Bold, too Busy, nor Babble [2] too long.

C too Courteous, too Cruel, nor Care too sorely.

D too Dull, too Dreading,[3] nor Drink too oft.

E too Elenge,[4] too Excellent,[5] nor too Earnest neither.

F too Fierce, too Familiar, but Friendly of cheer.

G too Glad, too (vain-)Glorious, and Gelousy [6] thou
    hate.

H too Hasty, too Hare-brained, nor too Heavy in thy
    Heart.

J too Jetting,[7] too Jangling,[8] nor Jape [9] not too oft.

K too Kind, too Keeping, and beware of Knaves' tricks.

L too Loth, too Loving, nor too Liberal of goods.

M too Meddling, too Merry, but as Measure asketh.

---

[1] Blame.   [2] Bourd = jest.
[3] Dreadful = full of dread.   [4] Melancholy. See note.
[5] "Superior," i.e., haughty. [6] Jealousy.
[7] Ostentatious.   [8] Chattering.   [9] Joke.

N too (an-)Noying, too Nice,[1] nor too New-fangled
    either.

O too Overbold, too Overthwart,[2] and hate thou Oaths.

P too Praising, too Privy [3] with Princes or dukes.

Q too Quaint, too Querulous, and Queme [4] thy master.

R too Riotous, too Revelling, nor Rage too Rudely.

S too Strange, too Stirring, nor Stare too strangely.

T too Toiling, too Tale-bearing, for Temperance is best.

V too Vengeful, too Envious, and (a-)Void all Villainy.

W too Wild, too Wrathful, nor Waste, nor Wade too
    deep.

    For a Measurable Mean is best for us all.

        Learn this or go Lacking.[5]

URBANITATIS [6]

WHOSO will of nurture know,
    Hark to me and I will show.
When you come before a lord,
In hall, in bower, or at board,
You must doff or cap or hood,

---

[1] Particular.
[2] Obstinate.
[3] In the confidence of.
[4] Please.
[5] Literally, be lewd (ignorant).
[6] *Of Politeness.*

Ere before him you have stood.
Twice or thrice beyond a doubt,
Before your sovereign must you lout [1] ;
On the right knee bend you low ;
For your own sake do ye so.
Hold your cap, forbear to don,
Till you're told to put it on.
All the while you speak with him,
Fair and lovely hold up your chin.
As bids the nurture of the book,
In his face straight shall you look.
Keep your hands still and your feet ;
To claw or trip it is not meet.[2]

. . . . . .

When into the hall you wend,
Among the gentles, good and hend [3]
Press not up high for any thing,
For noble blood or wit cunning.
Neither sit ye, neither lean,
For this is neither good nor clean.
Let not your countenance abate,[4]
For good nurture will save your state.

[1] Bow.   [2] Four lines omitted.   [3] Worthy.   [4] Be cast down.

If father, mother be right naught,
Happy the child that is well taught.
In hall, in chamber, mind you then :
Good manners always make good men.[1]
Look wisely to your betters ay,
Do them reverence as you may ;
But do ye none, sit all in row,
Unless ye them for betters know.
When you are set before the meat,
Fair and honestly it eat.
First, look ye that your hands be clean,
And that your knife be sharp and keen ;
Then cut your bread and all your meat,
Even when you set to eat.
If you sit by a worthier man
Than ye yourself well reckon can,
Suffer him first and do not let [2]
That he before you meat should get.
For the best piece do not strike [3]
Though you never so well it like.
Also keep your hands full well,
Not to 'file [4] the fair towél.

[1] See note.   [2] Hinder.   [3] Reach out.   [4] Defile.

Nor wipe your nose upon the cloth ;
To pick your teeth at meat be loth.
Nor in the cup too deeply sink,
Though ye have good will to drink,
Lest your eyen water thereby ;
For then it is no courtesy.
Look in your mouth there be no meat,
When you begin to drink or speak.
And when you see a man would drink,
Who heeds your carping,[1] you bethink,
And soon anon make end your tale,
Whether he drink wine or ale.
And look, ye scorn no man also,
In what degree ye see him go.
No man shall ye reprove or chide,
If ye in worship [2] would abide.
For words ye might speak out apace—
Should make you live in evil case.
Close your hand upon your fist,[3]
And keep you well from " Had I wist [4]—"
In chamber among the ladies bright,

[1] Chattering.   [2] Honour.
[3] See note.   [4] Known.   See note.

Keep your tongue and spend your sight.

Laugh not too loud with great outcry ;

Neither rage with ribaldry.

Play with none but with your peer,

And tell not all the tales you hear.

Discover [1] not your own [good] deed,

Neither for mirth, nor yet for meed.[2]

Gentle of speech—ye have your will ;

But foul of speech—ye fare full ill.

If ye follow a worthier man,

Than ye yourself well reckon can,

Let your right shoulder follow his back,[3]

For that is nurture ye must not lack.

When he speaks, then hold you still ;

When he has done, say then your will.

Be careful what you say or tell,

And in your speech advise you well.

Bereave [4] ye no man of his tale,

Neither at wine nor at ale.

Now may Christ of his sweet grace,

Give us all both wit and space

This [treatise] well to know and read,

[1] Make known.   [2] Reward.   [3] See note.   [4] Deprive.

And Heaven at last to have for meed.
Amen, Amen, so may it be.
So say we all for charity !

Explicit Tractus Urbanitatis.

THE LITTLE CHILDREN'S LITTLE BOOK

L ITTLE children, draw ye near
      And learn the courtesy written here ;
For clerks that well the Seven Arts know,[1]
Say Courtesy came to earth below,
When Gabriel hailed Our Lady by name,
And Elizabeth to Mary came.[1]
All virtues are closed [2] in courtesy,
And vices all in villainy.[1]
Look thy hands be washéd clean,
That no filth on thy nails be seen.
Take thou no meat till grace be said,
And till thou see all things arrayed.[3]
Look, my son, that thou not sit,
Till the ruler of the house thee bid.
And at thy meat, in the beginning,

[1] See note.   [2] Enclosed.   [3] Ready.

Look on poor men that thou think;[1]
For the full stomach ever faileth
To understand what the hungry aileth.
Eat not thy meat too hastily;
Abide and eat thou easily.
Till thou have thy full service,
Touch thou no mess [1] in no wise.
Carve thou not thy bread too thin,
Nor break it not in twain.
The morsels thou beginnest to touch
Cast them not into thy pouch.
Put not thy fingers in thy dish,
Neither in flesh, neither in fish.
Put not thy meat into the salt,
Into the cellar, that is a fault;[1]
But lay it fairly thee before,
Upon thy trencher, that is good lore.
Pick not thine ears nor thy nostrils;
If thou do, men will say thou come of churls.
And while thy meat in thy mouth is,
Drink thou not—forget not this.
Eat thy meat by small morsels too,

[1] See note.

Fill not thy mouth, as brothels [1] do.
Pick not thy teeth with thy knife.
In no company begin thou strife.
And when thou hast thy pottage done,
Out of thy dish thou put thy spoon.
Nor spit thou not over the table,
Nor thereupon—that is nothing able.[2]
Lay not thy elbow nor thy fist
Upon the table whiles thou eat'st.
Bulk [3] not, as a bean were in thy throat,
As a carl [4] that comes out of a cot.
If thy meat be of great price,
Beware of it, or thou art not wise.
Speak no word, nor still nor stark,[5]
And honour and courtesy look thou work.[6]
And at the table look thou make good cheer ;
Look thou whisper not in no man's ear.
With thy fingers [6] thou touch and taste
Thy meat, and look thou do no waste.
Look thou laugh not neither grin ;

[1] Churls.   [2] Seemly.   [3] Belch
[4] Churl; German, *kerl*, French, *carle*.
[5] Loud; literally, strong.   [6] See note.

And with much speech thou may'st do sin.

Meat nor drink look thou not spill,

But set it down, both fair and still.

Keep thy cloth clean thee beforn,

And bear thee so thou have no scorn.

Bite not thy meat, but carve it clean,

Be well aware no drop be seen.[1]

When thou eatest gape not too wide,

That thy mouth be seen on ilk a side.

And son, beware, I rede, of one thing :

Blow neither in thy meat nor in thy drink.

And if thy lord drink at that tide,

Drink thou not, but him abide ;

Be it at even, be it at noon,

Drink thou not till he have done.

Upon thy trencher no dirt must be ;

It is not honest as I tell thee.

Nor drink behind no man's back ; [1]

For if thou do, thou art to lack.

If cheese come forth, be not too greedy,

Nor to cut thereof too speedy.

Cast not thy bones unto the floor,

[1] See note.

But on thy trencher thee before.
Keep clean thy cloth before thee all,
And sit thou still, whatso befall,
Till grace be said unto the end,
And till thou have washen with thy friend.
Let him that worthier is than thou art,
Wash before thee; that is thy part.
And spit thou not in thy basin
My sweet son, that thou washest in.
And arise then up, full soft and still,
And jangle neither with Jack nor Jill.[1]
But take thy leave of the head lowly,
And thank him with thine heart highly,
And all the gentles together the same,[1]
And bare thee so thou have no blame.
Then will men thereafter say:
"A gentleman was here to-day."
And he that despiseth this teaching,
He is not worthy, without leasing,
Neither at good man's table to sit,
Nor of no worship for to wit.[2]
And therefore, children, for charity,

[1] See note. [2] Know.

Love this book though it little be,
And pray for him that made it thus,
That he may be helped by sweet Jesús,
To live and die among his friends,
And never to be cumbered with no fiends.[1]
And give us grace in joy to be,
Amen, Amen, for charity !
                    Explicit.
              Learn or be Lewd,
                            quoth Whytyng.
   Here endeth the Book of Courtesy that is full
necessary unto young children that must needs
learn the manner of courtesy.

THE YOUNG CHILDREN'S BOOK

WHOSO will thrive must be courteous, and learn
the virtues in his youth, or in his age he is out-
cast among men.   Clerks who know the Seven Sciences [1]
say that Courtesy came from heaven when Gabriel
greeted our Lady and Elizabeth met with her ; and
in it are included all virtues, as all vices in rudeness.

[1] See note.

Arise betimes from your bed, cross your breast and your forehead, wash your hands and face, comb your hair, and ask the grace of God to speed you in all your works ; then go to Mass and ask mercy for all your trespasses. Say " Good morning " courteously to whomsoever you meet by the way.

When ye have done, break your fast with good meat and drink, but before eating cross your mouth, your diet will be the better for it. Then say your grace—it occupies but little time—and thank the Lord Jesus for your food and drink. Say also a *Pater Noster* and an *Ave Maria* for the souls that lie in pain, and then go labour as you are bound to do. Be not idle, for Holy Scripture says to you of Christian faith that if you work, you must eat what you get with your hands.[1]   A man's arms are for working as a bird's wings for flying.

Look you be true in word and deed, the better shall you prosper ; for truth never works a man shame, but rather keeps him out of sin. The ways to Heaven are twain, mercy and truth, say clerks ; and he who will come to the life of bliss, must not fail to walk therein.

Make no promise save it be good, and then keep it

[1] See note.

with all your might, for every promise is a debt that must not be remitted through falsehood.

Love God and your neighbour, and thus may ye say without fear or dread that you keep all the law.

Uncalled go to no council, scorn not the poor, nor hurt any man, learn of him that can teach you, be no flatterer or scoffer, oppress not your servants, be not proud, but meek and gentle, and always walk behind your betters.

When your better shows his will, be silent; and in speaking to any man keep your hands and feet quiet, and look up into his face, and be always courteous.

Point not with your finger at anything, nor be lief [1] to tell tidings. If any man speak well of you or of your friends, he must be thanked. Have few words and wisely placed, for so may you win a good name.

Use no swearing or falsehood in buying or selling, else shall you be shamed at the last. Get your money honestly, and keep out of debt and sin. Be eager to please, and so live in peace and quiet.

Advise you well of whom you speak, and when and where and to whom.

[1] Ready, anxious.

Whenever you come unto a door, say, " God be here," ere you go further, and speak courteously, wherever you are, to sire or dame or their household.

Stand, and sit not down to meat until you are told by him that rules the hall; and do not change your seat, but sit upright and mannerly where he bids, and eat and drink and be fellowly, and share with him that sits by you—thus teaches Dame Courtesy.

Take your salt with a clean knife.

Be cool of speech and quarrel not, nor backbite a man who is away, but be glad to speak well of all. Hear and see and say nothing, then shall ye not be put to proof.

Hold you pleased with the meat and drink set before you, nor ask for better.   Wipe your mouth before you drink lest it foul the edge of the cup ; and keep your fingers, your lips and your chin clean, if you would win a good name.   When your meat is in your mouth, do not drink or speak or laugh—Dame Courtesy forbids. Praise your fare, wheresoever you be, for whether it be good or bad it must be taken in good part.

Whether you spit near or far, hold your hand before your mouth to hide it.

Keep your knife clean and sharp, and cleanse it on
some cut bread, not on the cloth, I bid you; a
courteous man is careful of the cloth. Do not put
your spoon in the dish or on the edge of it, as the untaught do, or make a noise when you sup as do boys.
Do not put the meat off your trencher into the dish,
but get a voider and empty it into that.

When your better hands you a cup, take it with both
hands lest it fall, and drink yourself and set it by; and
if he speaks to you, doff your cap and bow your knee.

Do not scratch yourself at the table so that men call
you a daw,[1] nor wipe your nose or nostrils, else men
will say you are come of churls. Make neither the cat
nor the dog your fellow at the table. And do not
play with the spoon, or your trencher, or your knife;
but lead your life in cleanliness and honest manners.

This book is made for young children that bide not
long at the school.[2] It may soon be conned and
learned, and will make them good if they be bad. God
give them grace to be virtuous, for so may they thrive.

Amen! quoth Kate.[2]

[1] Jackdaw.   [2] See note.

STANS PUER AD MENSAM[1]

MY dear son, first thyself enable
  With all thine heart to virtuous discipline ;
Afore thy sovereign, standing at the table,
  Dispose thou thyself, after my doctrine,
  To all nurture thy courage to incline.
First, let all recklessness in speaking cease,
And keep both hands and fingers still at peace.

Be simple of cheer, cast not thy look aside,
  Gaze not about, nor turn thy sight over all ;
Against the post let not thy back abide,
  Neither make thy mirror of the wall.
  Pick not thy nose, and most in speciál,
Be well aware and set hereon thy thought .
Before thy sovereign nor scratch nor pick thee nought.

Whoso speak to thee in any manner place,
  Lumpishly cast not thy head adown,
But with sober cheer look in his face ;
  Demurely walk through streets while in the town.

[1] *The Boy Standing at the Table.*

And take good heed of wisdom and renown,
That by no wanton laughing thou do no offence,
Before thy sovereign, while he is in presence.

Pare clean thy nails, and wash thy hands also,
    Before thy meat and when thou dost arise ;
Sit in that place thou art assignéd to,
    Press not too high in any manner wise.
    And when thy dinner served before thee lies,
Be not too hasty upon thy bread to bite,
Lest men of greediness should thee indict.[1]

Grinning and mowing [2] at the table eschew ;
    Cry not too loud ; honestly keep silence.
To stuff thy jaws with bread it is not due,
    With full mouth speak not, lest thou do offence.
    Drink not with bridle [3] for haste or negligence
Keep clean thy lips from fat of flesh or fish ;
Wipe fair thy spoon, nor leave it in thy dish.

Of bitten bread with thy teeth no sops think thou to make;
    Loud for to sup gainsays all gentleness.

[1] See note.   [2] Making faces.   [3] With mouth full of food.

With móuth imbrued [1] thy cup thou must not take,
    In ale, in wine, with hand leave no fatnéss ;
    Nor foul the napery through recklessness.
Beware that at the meat thou begin no strife.
Thy teeth at table pick not with no knife.

Of honest mirth let be thy dalliance,
    Swear no oaths and speak no ribaldry ;
The best morsels—have this in remembrance—
    Wholly thyself to take do not apply.
    Part with thy fellows, for that is courtesy.
Heap not thy trencher high with many morséls,
And from blackness alway keep thy nails.

Of courtesy it is against the law
    With rudeness, son, to make cause of offence ;
Of old forfeits [2] upbraid not thy fellów ;
    Toward thy sovereign do reverence.
    Play with no knife—take heed to my sentence.
At meat and at supper keep thee still and soft ;
Eke to and fro move not thy feet too oft.

---

[1] Stained with food.   [2] Offences.

Drop not thy breast with stew [1] and other pottáge,
 Bring no unscoured knives unto the table ;
Fill not thy spoon lest in the carriáge
 It spill aside, which were not commendáble.
 Be quick and ready, meek and serviceáble,
Well awaiting to fulfil anon
What that thy sovereign commandeth to be done.

And wheresoever thou be to dine or sup,
 Of gentleness, take salt with thy knife.·
And be well aware thou blow not in the cup.
 Reverence thy fellows, begin with them no strife.
 To thy power keep peace all thy life.
Interrupt no man, whereso that thou wend,
No man in his tale, till he have made an end.

With thy fingers mark thou not thy tale.
 Be well advised, and namely, in tender age,
To drink measurably both wine and ale.
 Be not too copious of thy languáge.
 As time requireth, show not thy viságe
Too glad nor sorry, but keep thee even between,
For loss, or lucre, or any case suddén.

[1] Harleian MS., sauce.

Be soft [1] in measure, not hasty but tractáble ;
  Over-soft is nought, in no manner thing.
To children belongeth not to be vengeáble,[2]
  Soon movéd and full soon again fighting ; [3]
  And as it is remembered by writing :
Wrath of children is soon overgone ;
With the parts of an apple they be made at one.[4]

In children war is now mirth and now debate ;
  In their quarrel is no great violence ;
Now play, now weeping, and seldom in one estate,
  To their complaints give never any credénce.
  A rod reformeth all their negligence.
In their courage [5] no rancour doth abide.
Who that spareth the rod all virtues sets aside.

Ah, little ballad, void of eloquence,[6]
  I pray young children that thee shall see and read,
Though thou be copious of sentence,

[1] Harl. MS., meek.   [2] Revengeful.
[3] Harl. MS., forgiving.
[4] Harl. MS., With an apple the parties be made at one.
[5] Heart.   [6] See note.

Yet to thy clauses for to take heed,
Which into all virtue shall their youth lead.
In this writing, though there be no date,
    If aught be amiss in word, syllable or deed,
I submit me to correction without any debate.

HOW THE GOOD WIFE TAUGHT
HER DAUGHTER

THE good wife taught her daughter,
    Full many a time and oft,
A full good woman to be ;
For said she : " Daughter to me dear,
Something good now must thou hear,
    If thou wilt prosper thee.

Daughter, if thou wilt be a wife,
    Look wisely that thou work ;
Look lovely and in good life,
    Love God and Holy Kirk.[1]
Go to church whene'er thou may,
    Look thou spare for no rain,

[1] See note.

For best thou farest on that day ;
    To commune with God be fain.
      He must needs well thrive,
      That liveth well all his life,[1]
        My lief [2] child.

Gladly give thy tithes and thy offerings both,
To the poor and the bed-rid—look thou be not loth.
Give of thine own goods and be not too hard,
For seldom is the house poor where God is stewárd.
      Well is he provéd
      Who the poor hath lovéd,
        My lief child.

When thou sittest in the church, o'er thy beads bend ;
Make thou no jangling with gossip or with friend.
Laugh thou to scorn neither old body nor young,
But be of fair bearing and of good tongue.
      Through thy fair bearing
      Thy worship hath increasing,
        My lief child.

[1] See note.   [2] Dear.

If any man offer thee courtship, and would marry thee,
Look that thou scorn him not, whatsoever he be ; [1]
But show it to thy friends and conceal it naught.
Sit not by him nor stand where sin might be wrought,
    For a slander raised of ill
    Is evil for to still,
        My lief child.

The man that shall thee wed before God with a ring,
Love thou him and honour most of earthly thing.
Meekly thou him answer and not as an atterling,[2]
So may'st thou slake his mood,[3] and be his dear darling.
    A fair word and a meek
    Doth anger slake,
        My lief child.

Fair of speech shalt thou be, glad and of mild mood,
True in word and in deed, and in conscience good.
Keep thee from sin, from villainy and from blame ;
And look thou bear thee so that none say of thee shame,
    For he that in good life hath run,
    Full oft his weal hath won,
        My lief child.

[1] See note.   [2] Shrew. See note.   [3] Quiet his wrath.

Be of seemly semblance, wise, and other good cheer ;
Change not thy countenance for aught that thou may
    hear.
Fare not as a gig,[1] for nought that may betide.
Laugh thou not too loud nor yawn thou not too wide.
        But laugh thou soft and mild,
          And be not of cheer too wild,
            My lief child.

And when thou goest on thy way, go thou not too fast,
Brandish not with thy head, nor with thy shoulders cast,[2]
Have not too many words, from swearing keep aloof,
For all such manners come to an evil proof.
        For he that catcheth to him an evil name,
          It is to him a foul fame,
            My lief child.

Go thou not into the town, as it were agaze,[3]
From one house to another, for to seek the maze ; [4]
Nor to sell thy russet,[5] to the market shalt thou go,
And then to the tavern to bring thy credit low.

---

[1] Giddy girl.   [2] Shake or shrug.
[3] See note.   [4] Wonder ?   See note.
[5] Coarse brown stuff, homespun, frieze.

For they that taverns haunt
From thrift soon come to want,
    My lief child.

And if thou be in any place where good ale is aloft,[1]
Whether that thou serve thereof or that thou sit soft,
Measurably thou take thereof, that thou fall in no blame,
For if thou be often drunk, it falleth to thy shame.
    For those that be often drunk—
    Thrift is from them sunk,
        My lief child.

Go not to the wrestling or shooting at the cock,[2]
As it were a strumpet or a gigggelot[3] ;
Dwell at home, daughter, and love thy work much,
And so thou shalt, my lief child, wax the sooner rich.
    A merry thing 'tis evermore,
    A man to be served of his own store,
        My lief child.

Acquaint thee not with each man that goeth by the
    street,
Though any man speak to thee, swiftly[4] thou him greet;

[1] A-going.   [2] See note.
[3] A giggling girl, expressively spelled.   [4] Curtly.

By him do not stand, but let him his way depart,
Lest he by his villainy should tempt thy heart.
> For all men be not true
> That fair words can shew,
> > My lief child.

Also, for covetousness gifts beware to take;
Unless thou know why else,[1] quickly them forsake;
For with gifts may men soon women overcome,
Though they were as true as steel or as stone.
> Bound forsooth is she
> That of any man takes fee,[2]
> > My lief child.

And wisely govern thy house, and serving maids and men,
Be thou not too bitter or too debonaire with them;
But look well what most needs to be done,
And set thy people at it, both rathely[3] and soon.
> For ready is at need
> A foredone[4] deed,
> > My lief child.

---

[1] Another reason.   [2] Gift.
[3] Quickly.   [4] Done betimes.

And if thy husband be from home, let not thy folk do ill,
But look who doeth well and who doeth nil ;
And he that doeth well, quit him well his while,
But he that doeth other, serve him as the vile.

> A foredone deed
> Will another speed,[1]
> > My lief child.

And if thy time be strait and great be thy need,
Then like a housewife set to work with speed ;
Then will they all do better that about thee stand,
For work is sooner done that hath full many a hand.

> For many a hand and wight
> Makes a heavy work light ;
> And after thy good service,
> Thy name shall arise,
> > My lief child.

Whate'er thy household doth, about them must thou
    wend,
And as much as thou mayest, be at that one end,
If thou find any fault, make them soon amend,
As they have time and space, and may them defend.

[1] See note.

To compel a deed be done, if there be no space,
It is but tyranny, without temperance and grace,
    My lief child.

And look that all things be well when they their work
    forsake,
Forget thou not the keys into thy ward to take
And beware to whom thou trustest, and for no fancy
    spare,
For much harm hath fallen to them that be not 'ware.
    But, daughter, look thou be wise, and do as I
        thee teach,
        And trust none better than thyself, for no fair
            speech,
            My lief child.

And give your household their hire at their term-day,[1]
Whether they dwell still with thee, or they wend away.
Do well by them of the goods thou hast in hold,
And then shall they say well of thee, both the young
    and old.
    Thy good name to thy friends
    Great joy and gladness lends,
        My lief child.

[1] See note.

And if thy neighbour's wife hath on rich attire,
Therefore mock not, nor let scorn burn thee as a fire.
But thank thou God in heaven for what He may thee give,
And so shalt thou, my daughter dear, a good life live,
  He hath ease in his power,
  Who thanks the Lord every hour,
   My lief child.

Housewifely thou shalt go on the working day,
For pride, rest, and idleness take thrift away;
But when the Holy Day is come, well clothéd shalt
  thou be,
The Holy Day to honour, and God will cherish thee.
  Have in mind to worship God alway,
  For much pride comes of the evil day,
   My lief child.

When thou art a wife, a neighbour for to be,
Love then well thy neighbours as God hath com-
  manded thee.
It behoveth thee so for to do,
And to do to them as thou wouldst be done to.
  If any discord happen, night or day,
  Make it no worse, mend it if thou may,
   My lief child.

And if thou art a rich wife, be not then too hard,
But welcome fair thy neighbours that come to-thee-
ward
With meat, drink, and honest cheer, such as thou
mayest bid,[1]
To each man after his degree, and help the poor at need.
    And also for hap that may betide,
      Please well thy neighbours that dwell thee beside,
        My lief child.

Daughter, look that thou beware, whatsoever thee
betide,
Make not thy husband poor with spending or with pride.
A man must spend as he may that hath but easy good,[2]
For as a wren hath veins, men must let her blood.[3]
    His thrift waxeth thin
    That spendeth ere he win,
      My lief child.

Borrow not too busily, nor take thine hire first,
This may make the more need, and end by being worst.
Nor make thee not to seem rich with other men's store,
Therefore spend thou never a farthing more.

[1] Offer.   [2] Moderate means.   [3] See note.

For though thou borrow fast,
It must home again at last,
        My lief child.

And if thy children be rebel and will not bow them low,
If any of them misdo, neither curse them nor blow;[1]
But take a smart rod and beat them in a row,
Till they cry mercy and their guilt well know.
        Dear child, by this lore
        They will love thee ever more,
            My lief child.

And look to thy daughters that none of them be lorn;
From the very time that they are of thee born,
Busy thyself and gather fast for their marriage,
And give them to spousing, as soon as they be of age.
        Maidens be fair and amiable,
        But in their love full unstable,
            My lief child.

Now have I taught thee, daughter, as my mother did me;
Think thereon night and day, that forgotten it not be.

[1] Scold.

Have measure and lowness, as I have thee taught,
Then whatever man shall wed thee will regret it naught.
  Better you were a child unbore
  Than untaught in this wise lore,
   My lief child.

Now thrift and speed be thine, my sweet bairn [near
  or far]!
Of all our former fathers that ever were or are,
Of all patriarchs and prophets that ever were alive,—
Their blessing may'st thou have, and well may'st thou
  thrive!
  For well it is with that child
  That with sin is not defiled,
   My lief child.

The blessing of God may'st thou have, and of His
  mother bright,
Of all angels and archangels and every holy wight![1]
And may'st thou have grace to wend thy way full right,
To the bliss of heaven, where God sits in His might!
        Amen.

[1] Creature.

HOW THE WISE MAN TAUGHT HIS SON

LISTEN, lordlings, and ye shall hear how the wise man taught his son. Take good heed to this matter and learn it if ye can, for this song was made with good intent to make men true and steadfast, and a thing well begun makes often a good ending.

There was a wise man taught his son while he was yet a child of tender years, meek and fair to look upon, very eager for learning and with a great desire to all goodness; and his father taught him well and featly by good example and fair words.

He said: " My son, take good heed every morning, ere ye do worldly thing, lift up your heart to God, and pray as devoutly as you can for grace to lead a good life, and to escape sin both night and day, and that heaven's bliss may be your meed.

" And, my son, wherever you go, be not full of tales; beware what you say, for your own tongue may be your foe. If you say aught, take good heed where and to whom, for a word spoken to-day may be repented seven years after.

" And, son, whatever manner of man ye be, give yourself not to idleness, but busy yourself every day according to your estate. Beware of rest and ease, which things nourish sloth. Ever to be busy, more or less, is a full good sign of honesty.[1]

" And, son, I warn you also not to desire to bear office, for then can it be no other than that you must either displease and hurt your neighbours, or else forswear yourself and not do as your office demands ; and get yourself, *maugré*,[2] here and there, an hundredfold more than thanks.

" And, son, as far as you may, go on no evil quests, nor bear false witness in any man's matter. It were better for you to be deaf and dumb than to enter wrongfully into a quest. Think, son, on the dreadful doom that God shall deem [3] us at the last !

" And, son, of another thing I warn you, on my blessing take good heed of tavern-haunting, and of the dice, and flee all lechery, lest you come to an evil end, for it will lead astray all your wits and bring you into great mischief.

" And, son, sit not up too long at even, or have late

[1] Truth, literally.   [2] In spite of yourself.   [3] Judge.

De la disputation q̃ fist
Cathon a soy mesmes
et contre son corpz a sa
mort

suppers, though ye be strong and hale, for with such outrage your health shall worsen. And of late walking comes debate,[1] and of sitting and drinking out of time, therefore beware and go to bed betimes and wink.

"And, son, if ye would have a wife, take her not for her money, but inquire wisely of all her life, and give good heed that she be meek, courteous and prudent, even though she be poor ; and such an one will do you more good service in time of need, than a richer.

"And if your wife be meek and good, and serve you well and pleasantly, look ye be not so mad as to charge her too grievously, but rule her with a fair hand and easy, and cherish her for her good deeds. For a thing unskilfully overdone makes needless grief to grow, and it is better to have a meal's meat of homely fare with peace and quiet, than an hundred dishes with grudging and much care. And therefore learn this well that if you want a wife to your ease, take her never the more for the riches she may have, though she might endow you with lands.

"And ye shall not displease your wife, nor call her by no villainous names, for it is a shame to you to mis-

[1] Strife.

call a woman; and in so doing, ye are not wise, for if ye defame your own wife, no wonder that another should do so! Soft and fair will tame alike hart and hind, buck and doe.

" On the other hand, be not too hasty to fight or chide, if thy wife come to you at any time with complaint of man or child; and be not avenged till you know the truth, for you might make a stir in the dark, and afterwards it should rue you both.

" And, son, if you be well at ease, and sit warm among your neighbours, do not get new-fangled ideas, or be hasty to change, or to flit; [1] for if ye do, ye lack wit and are unstable, and men will speak of it and say : ' This fool can bide nowhere ! '

" And, son, the more goods you have, the rather bear you meekly, and be humble, and boast not overmuch; it is wasted, for by their boasting men know fools.

" And look you pay well what you owe, and set no great store by other riches, for death takes both high and low, and then—farewell, all that there is ! And therefore do by my counsel, and take example from other men, how little their goods avail them when

[1] Move house (Scotch still).

they be dolven [1] in their dens; [2] and one that was
not of his kin hath his wife, and all that there is.[3]

"Son, keep you from deadly sin, and assay to enter
Paradise. Make amends for your trespasses and deal
out of your goods to poor men, make friends of your
foes, and strive to gain salvation for your soul, for the
world is false and frail, and every day doth worsen.
Son, set nought by this world's weal, for it fares as a
ripe cherry. And death is ever, I trow, the most certain thing that is; and nothing is so uncertain as to
know the time thereof. Therefore, my son, think on
this, on all that I have said, and may Jesus, who for us
bare the crown of thorns, bring us to His bliss."

AMEN.

JOHN RUSSELL'S BOOK OF NURTURE

" IN nomine Patris, God keep me, et Filii, for charity,
Et Spiritus Sancti, where that I go by land or
else by sea !
An usher I am ye may behold to a prince of high degree,
That enjoys to inform and teach all those that would
thrive in prosperity."

---

[1] Buried.   [2] Graves   [3] See note.

Should I meet with any man who either through in-experience or through negligence knows naught of such things as I shall hereafter diligently show, for my conscience' sake I will instruct him ; for methinks it is charitable to teach virtue and good manners, in which most youths are barren and dull. But if there be any who can nothing good and are not willing to learn, give them a bauble to play with, for they will never thrive.

" As I rose out of my bed, in a merry season of May,
To sport me in a forest, where sights were fresh and gay,
I met with the forester ; I prayed him to say me not nay,
That in his woodland I might walk among the deer away.
As I wandered at will, in the wood that was so green,
There lay three herds of deer, a seemly sight, I ween.
I beheld on my right hand the sun that shone so sheen;
I saw where walked a seemly young man, that slender
      was and lean.
His bow he took in hand toward the deer to stalk,
I prayed him his shot to leave and softly with me to walk."

Thereupon the young man was glad and loved to

talk with me ; but when I inquired whom he served, he said : " God help me, sir, I serve myself and else no other man."

" Is thy governance good [1] ? " I said. " My son, tell me if thou wilt."

" I would I were out of this world," said he; " I reck not how soon when ! "

" Say not so, good son, beware ! Methinks you mean amiss for God forbids wanhope,[2] which is a horrible sin. Therefore, good son, open your heart to me, peradventure I can relieve you. Remember that when bale [3] is highest, boot [3] is nighest."

" In truth, sir, I have sought far and near in many a wildsome way to get me a master. But because I knew nothing good, and showed this wherever I went, every man denied me ; day by day, wanton [4] and over-nice, reckless, lewd and chattering like a jay, every man refused me."

" Now, good son, if I will teach, will you learn ? Will you be a serving-man, a ploughman, a labourer, a courtier, a clerk, a merchant, a mason or an artificer, a chamberlain, a butler, a panter or a carver ? "

[1] See note.   [2] Lack of hope, *i.e.*, despair.
[3] Evil—help.   [4] Ill-bred.

"Teach me, sir, the duties of a butler, a panter or a chamberlain, and especially, the cunning of a carver. If you will make me to know all these, I will pray for your soul that it come never in pain ! "

" Son, I will teach you with right good will, so as you will love and fear God as is right and proper, be true to yqur master, and not waste his goods, but love and fear him, and duly fulfil his commandments."

The Duties of a Panter or Butler

" The first year, my son, you shall be panter or butler. In the pantry, you must always keep three sharp knives, one to chop the loaves, another to pare them, and a third, sharp and keen, to smooth and square the trenchers with.[1]

" Always cut your lord's bread, and see that it be new ; and all other bread at the table one day old ere you cut it, all household bread three days old, and trencher-bread four days old.

" Look that your salt be fine, white, fair, and dry ; and have your salt-plane of ivory, two inches

[1] See note.

wide and three long; and see to it that the lid of the
salt-cellar touch not the salt.

"Good son, look that your napery be sweet and
clean, and that your table-cloth, towel, and napkin be
folded neatly, your table-knives brightly polished and
your spoons fair washed—ye wot well what I mean.

"Look ye have two wine-augers, a greater and a less,
some gutters of boxwood that fit them, also a gimlet to
pierce with, a tap and a bung, ready to stop the flow
when it is time.   So when you broach a pipe, good son,
do after my teaching : pierce or bore with an auger or
gimlet, slanting upward, four fingers' breadth from the
lower rim, so as not to cause the lees to rise—I warn
you especially."

[Here follows a list of fruits and preserves, which
presently becomes a mere dietary, ll. 73–108.]

"Take good heed to the wines, red, white, and sweet;
look to them every night with a candle, to see that
they neither ferment nor leak.   Never forget to wash
the heads of the pipes with cold water every night ; and
always carry a gimlet, adze and linen clouts,[1] large and
small.   If the wine ferment, ye shall know by its sing

1 See note.

ing, so keep at hand a pipe of *couleur de rose*,[1] that has
been spent in drinking and add to the fermentation the
dregs of this, and it shall be amended.   If sweet wine
be sick or pallid, put in a Romney to improve it."

[Then follows a list of the sweet wines, and a long
recipe for *Hippocras*, ll. 117–176.]

The Buttery

" See that your cups and pots be clean, both within
and without.   Serve no ale till it is five days old, for
new ale is wasteful.[1]   And look that all things about
you be sweet and clean.

" Be fair of answer, ready to serve, and gentle of
cheer, and then men will say ; ' There goes a gentle
officer.'

" Beware that ye give no person stale drink, for fear
that ye bring many a man into disease for many a year.[1]

" My son, it is now the time of day to lay the table.
First, wipe it with a cloth ere it be spread, then lay on
it a cloth called a *cowche*.[1]   You take one end and your
mate the other, and draw it straight ; and lay a second

[1] See note.

cloth with its fold on the outer edge of the table.[1]
Lift the upper part and let it hang even. And then
lay the third cloth with its fold on the inner edge,
making a *state*[1] half a foot wide, with the top.
Cover your ewery-cupboard [2] with a diapered-towel,
and put a towel round your neck,[1] for that is courtesy,
and put one end of it mannerly over your left arm ; and
on the same arm place your lord's napkin, and on it lay
eight loaves of bread, with three or four trencher-
loaves. Take one end of the towel in your left hand,
as the manner is, together with the salt-cellar—look
you do this—and take the other end of the towel in
your right hand with the spoons and knives.

" Set the salt on your lord's right hand, and to the
left of your salt, one or two trenchers, and to the left
again, your knife by itself and plain to see, and the
white rolls, and beside them a spoon upon a fair folded
napkin. Cover your spoon, napkin, trencher and knife,
so that they cannot be seen ; and at the other end of
the table place a salt with two trenchers.

[1] See note.
[2] A cupboard in which were kept the jugs (ewers) and
basins used in washing, before and after meals.

" If you wish to wrap up your lord's bread in a
stately fashion, first square off the bread sharply and
evenly, and see that no bun or loaf be larger in propor-
tion to the others, and so shall ye be able to wrap it up
mannerly for your master. Take a towel of Rennes
cloth,[1] two and a half yards long, fold it lengthwise [1]
and lay it on the table. Roll up a handful from each
end tightly and stiffly, then in the middle of the towel
place eight loaves or buns, bottom to bottom, and then
wrap them wisely and skilfully. To tell you more
plainly for your information: take the ends of the towel
that lies on the bread, draw them out and twist tightly
a handful nearest the bread and smooth the wrapper
stiffly. When it is ready, you must open one end all
in a moment before your lord.

When your sovereign's table is dressed in this array,
place salts on all the other tables, and lay trenchers
and cups; and then set out your cupboard with gay
silver and silver-gilt, and your ewery board with basins
and ewers, and hot and cold water, each to temper the
other. Look that you have ever enough napkins,
spoons and cups for your lord's table; also, for your

[1] See note.

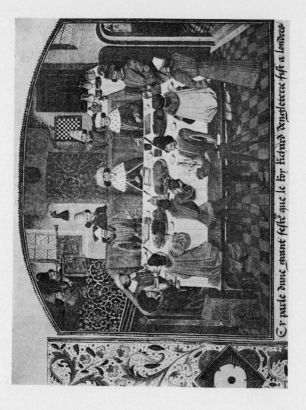

Cy parle dune grant feste que le Roy Richard Denglleterre fyst a londres

own dignity, that your pots for ale and wine be as clean as possible, and beware ever of flies and motes, for your own sake.

" With lowly courtesy, make the surnape [1] with a cloth under a double of fair napery ; fold the two ends of the towel to the outer edge of the cloth, and so hold the three ends together ; then fold them all so that there is a pleat at about a foot's distance, and lay it fair and smooth for your lord to wash after meat, if he will. At the right side of the table, you must guide it along, and the marshal must slip it further—the right side up of all three cloths—and let it be drawn straight and even, both in length and breadth ; then raise the upper part of the towel and lay it without wrinkling straight to the other side so that half a yard or an ell hangs down at each end, where the sewer [1] may make a *state*, and so please his master. When your lord has washed, you must take up the surnape with your two arms, and carry it back to the ewery yourself.

" Carry a towel about your neck when serving your lord, bow to him, uncover your bread and set it by the salt. Look that all have knives, spoons and napkins,

[1] See note.

and always when you pass your lord, see that you bow
your knees.

" Go forth to the *port-payne* [1] and there take eight
loaves, and put four at each end of the table, and be
sure that each person has a spoon and a napkin.

" Watch the sewer to see how many pottages he
covers, and do ye for as many, and serve each according
to his degree ; and see that none lack bread, ale or wine.

" Be glad of cheer, courteous of knee, soft of speech ;
have clean hands and nails and be carefully dressed.

" Do not cough or spit or retch too loud, or put
your fingers into the cups to seek bits of dust.

" Have an eye to all grumbling and fault-finding, and
prevent backbiting of their fellows among the lords at
meat, by serving all with bread, ale and wine ; and so
shall ye have of all men good love and praise."

Simple Conditions

" I will that ye eschew forever the ' simple conditions ' of a person that is not taught.

" Do not claw your head or your back as if you

[1] Bread-carrier, apparently a sort of tray, *lintheum panarium*,
an ell long and a yard wide.

were after a flea, or stroke your hair as if you sought
a louse.

"Be not glum,[1] nor twinkle with your eyes, nor be
heavy of cheer; and keep your eyes free from winking
and watering.[2]

"Do not pick your nose or let it drop clear pearls,
or sniff, or blow it too loud, lest your lord hear.

"Twist not your neck askew like a jackdaw; wring
not your hands with picking or trifling or shrugging,
as if ye would saw [wood]; nor puff up your chest,
nor pick your ears, nor be slow of hearing.

"Retch not, nor spit too far, nor laugh or speak too
loud. Beware of making faces and scorning; and be
no liar with your mouth. Nor yet lick your lips or
drivel.

"Do not have the habit of squirting or spouting
with your mouth, or gape, or yawn, or pout. And do
not lick a dish with your tongue to get out dust.

"Be not rash or reckless—that is not worth a clout.

"Do not sigh with your breast, or cough, or breathe
hard in the presence of your sovereign, or hiccough, or
belch, or groan never the more. Do not trample with

[1] Text: *glowting*.   [2] See note.

your feet, or straddle your legs, or scratch your body—
there is no sense in showing off. Good son, do not
pick your teeth, or grind, or gnash them, or with
puffing and blowing cast foul breath upon your lord.
. . . These gallants in their short coats—that is ungoodly guise. Other faults on this matter, I spare not
to disapprove in my opinion, when [a servant] is waiting on his master at table. Every sober sovereign must
despise all such things.

" A man might find many more conditions than are
named here ; but let every honest servant avoid them
for his own credit.

" Panter, yeoman of the cellar, butler and ewerer, I
will that ye obey the marshal, sewer and carver."

" Good sir, I pray you teach me the skill of carving,
and the fair handling of a knife, and all the ways that
I shall break open, unlace and penetrate all manner of
fowl, flesh and fish—how I shall demean me with each."

[Office of a Carver]

" My son, thy knife must be clean and bright ; and
it beseems thee to have thy hands fair washed. Hold
always thy knife surely, so as not to hurt thyself, and

have not more than two fingers and the thumb on thy keen knife.

" Midway in thy hand, set the end of thy haft firmly ; and unlace and mince with the thumb and two fingers only. In cutting and placing bread, and voiding of crumbs and trencher, look you have skill with two fingers and the thumb. Likewise, never use more for fish, flesh, beast or fowl—that is courtesy.

" Touch no manner of meat with thy right hand, but with thy left, as is proper. Always with thy left hand grasp the loaf with all thy might ; and hold thy knife firmly, as I have instructed thee. Ye do not right to soil your table, nor to wipe your knives on that, but on your napkin.

" First take a loaf of trenchers in your left hand, then your table-knife, as I have said before ; and with its edge raising your trencher up by you as near the point as you may, lay it before your lord. Right so set four trenchers, one by another, four square, and upon them a single trencher alone. And take your loaf of light bread, as I have told you, and cut with the edge of the knife near your hand ; first pare the quarters of the loaf round all about, and cut the upper crust [1] for your lord, and bow to him ; and suffer the other part to remain still at the bottom, and so nigh spent out,[2] and lay him of the crumbs a quarter of the loaf.

"Touch not the loaf after it is so trimmed ; put it on a platter or on the beforenamed almsdish. Make clean your board that ye be not blamed ; and so shall the sewer serve his lord, and neither of you be vexed."

[Here follows a list of *Fumosities*, indigestibilities, as Dr. Furnivall calls them, ll. 349–68. The young man then says :]

"Now fair befal you, father, and well may ye [a]chieve
For these points by practice I hope full well to prove ;
And yet shall I pray for you daily while that I live,
Both for body and soul that God you guide from grief."

[He then begs to be taught the art of "carving of fish and flesh [1] after the cook's care," and receives detailed instructions for every sort of food, roasted, baked and fried, for the serving of soups, making of sauces and carving of fish, ll. 377–649. He then says :]

[1] See note.   [2] Used up.

" Now, father, fair fall ye, and Christ you have in cure,
For of the nurture of carving, I suppose that I be sure.
But yet another office there is, save I dare not endure
To ask you any further, for fear of displeasure.
For to be a sewer I would I had the cunning,
Then durst I do my devoir [1] with any worshipful to be
        woning ; [2]
Since that I know the course and the craft of carving,
I would see the sight of a sewer, what way he showeth
        in serving."

Office of a Sewer

" Now since, my son, you wish to learn this science,
dread nothing of great difficulty ; I will gladly teach
you, if you will but listen.

" Take heed when the worshipful head of any household has washed before meat and begins to say grace,
then hie you to the kitchen where the servants must
attend and take your orders. First ask the panter or
officer of the spicery for fruits, such as butter, plums,
damsons, grapes and cherries, which are served before
dinner according to the season to make men merry, and

[1] Duty.   [2] Dwelling.

ask if any such are to be served that day.   Then com-
mune with the cook and surveyor [1] as to what meats
and how many dishes are prepared.   When they two
have agreed with you, then must the cook dress up all
dishes to the surveying-board,[2] and the surveyor must
soberly and without turmoil deliver up the dishes to
you, that you may convey them to your lord.   When
you are at the board of service, see that you have
courtly and skilful officers to prevent any dish being
stolen, which might easily cause a scandal to arise in
your service as sewer.   See that you have proper servants to carry the dishes, marshals, squires and ser-
jeants-at-arms, if they be there, to bring the dishes
without delay or injury from the kitchen, and you need
not fear to set them on the table yourself." [3]

[Then follow various menus, ll. 686-858.   The
young man answers :]

" Now fair fall you, father, in faith, I am full fain ;
For lovesomely ye have taught me this nurture again.

---

[1] On the office, see p. 106 below.
[2] *Sideboard* is perhaps the nearest equivalent.
[3] See note.

Pleaseth it you to certify me with one word or twain,
The courtesy to conceive conveniently for every
 chamberlain ? "

The Office of a Chamberlain

" The duty of a chamberlain is to be diligent in office,
neatly clad, his clothes not torn, hands and face well
washed and head well kempt.

" He must be ever careful—not negligent—of fire and
candle. And look you [1] give diligent attendance to
your master, be courteous, glad of cheer, quick of hearing in every way, and be ever on the lookout for things
to do him pleasure ; if you will acquire these qualities,
it may advance you well.

" See that your lord has a clean shirt and hose, a
short coat,[2] a doublet, and a long coat, if he wear such,
his hose well brushed, his socks at hand, his shoes or
slippers as brown as a water-leech.[1]

" In the morning, against your lord shall rise, take
care that his linen be clean, and warm it at a clear fire,
not smoky, if [the weather] be cold or freezing.

[1] See note.   [2] Tunic or shirt, lit. *petticoat*.

"When he rises make ready the foot-sheet, and forget not to place a chair or some other seat with a cushion on it before the fire, with another cushion for the feet. Over the cushion and chair spread this sheet so as to cover them ; and see that you have a kerchief and a comb to comb your lord's head before he is fully dressed.

"Then pray your lord in humble words to come to a good fire and array him thereby, and there to sit or stand pleasantly ; and wait with due manners to assist him. First hold out to him his tunic, then his doublet while he puts in his arms, and have his stomacher well aired to keep off harm, as also his vamps [1] and socks, and so shall he go warm all day.

"Then draw on his socks and his hose by the fire, and lace or buckle his shoes, draw his hosen on well and truss them up to the height that suits him, lace his doublet in every hole, and put round his neck and on his shoulders a kerchief ; and then gently comb his head with an ivory comb, and give him water wherewith to wash his hands and face.

[1] Short stockings, that covered the feet, and reached to the ankle, just above the shoe (*avant-pied*).

" Then kneel down on your knee and say thus :
' Sir, what robe or gown doth it please you to wear
to-day ? ' Then get him such as he asks for, and hold
it out for him to put on, and do on his girdle, if he
wear one, tight or loose, arrange his robe in the proper
fashion, give him a hood or hat for his head, a cloak
or *cappe-de-huse*,[1] according as it be fair or foul, or all
misty with rain ; and so shall ye please him.   Before
he goes out, brush busily about him, and whether he
wear satin, sendal,[2] velvet, scarlet[3] or grain,[4] see that
all be clean and nice.

" If he be prince or prelate or other potentate,
before he go to church see that all things for the pew
be made ready, and forget not cushion, carpet, curtain,
beads or book.

" Then return in haste to your lord's chamber, strip
the clothes off the bed and cast them aside, and beat
the feather-bed, but not so as to waste any feathers, and
see that the blankets and sheets be clean.   When you
have made the bed mannerly, cover it with a coverlet,
spread out the bench-covers,[5] and cushions, set up the

---

[1] Cap or cape to wear in the house.   [2] A kind of silk.
[3] Scarlet cloth.   [4] Crimson cloth.   [5] See note.

head-sheet [1] and pillow, and remove the basin. See
that carpets [2] be laid round the bed and dress the windows, and the cupboard with carpets [2] and cushions.
See there be a good fire conveyed into the chamber,
with plenty of wood and fuel to make it up.

"The Wardrobe

" You must attend busily to your lord's wardrobe,
to keep the clothes well, and to brush them cleanly.
Use a soft brush, and remember that overmuch brush-
ing easily wears out cloth.

" Never let woollen clothes or furs go a sevennight
without being brushed or shaken, for moths be always
ready to alight in them and engender ; so always keep
an eye on drapery and skinnery.

" If your lord take a nap after his meal to digest his
stomach, have ready kerchief and comb, pillow and
head-sheet ; yet be not far from him—take heed what
I say—for much sleep is not good in the middle of the

---

[1] Sheet at the head of the bed.

[2] First, carpets ; second, tapestries. The *Book of Courtesy*
has *tapetis*, Fr. *tapis*.

day, and have ready water and towel so that he may
wash after his sleep.

" When he has supped and goes to his chamber,
spread forth your foot-sheet, as I have already shown
you, take off his gown or whatever garment by the
license of his estate he wears,[1] and lay it up in such
place as ye best know. Put a mantle on his back to
keep his body from cold, set him on the foot-sheet,
made ready as I have directed, and pull off his shoes,
socks and hosen, and throw these last over your shoulder,
or hold them on your arm. Comb his hair, but first
kneel down, and put on his kerchief and nightcap
wound [1] in seemly fashion. Have the bed, head-sheet
and pillow ready; and when he is in bed, there to
sleep safe and sound, draw the curtains round about
the bed, set there his night-light with wax or Paris-
candle,[1] and see that there is enough to last the night,
drive out the dog and the cat, giving them a clout,
take no leave of your lord, but bow low to him and
retire, and thus shall ye have thanks and reward
whensoever it fall.

[1] See note.

"*A Bath or Stew so-called*

"If your lord wishes to bathe and wash his body clean, hang sheets round the roof, every one full of flowers and sweet green herbs, and have five or six sponges to sit or lean upon, and see that you have one big sponge to sit upon, and a sheet over so that he may bathe there for a while, and have a sponge also for under his feet, if there be any to spare, and always be careful that the door is shut. Have a basin full of hot fresh herbs and wash his body with a soft sponge, rinse him with fair warm rose-water, and throw it over him ; then let him go to bed ; but see that the bed be sweet and nice ; and first put on his socks and slippers that he may go near the fire and stand on his foot-sheet, wipe him dry with a clean cloth, and take him to bed to cure his troubles.

"*The Making of a Medicinable Bath*

" Boil together hollyhock,[1] mallow, wall pellitory and brown fennel, danewort, St. John's wort, centaury, ribwort and camomile, heyhove, heyriff, herb-benet,

[1] See note on these various herbs.

bresewort, smallage, water speedwell, scabious, bugloss (?), and wild flax which is good for aches— boil withy leaves and green oats together with them, and throw them hot into a vessel and put your lord over it and let him endure for a while as hot as he can, being covered over and closed on every side; and whatever disease, grievance or pain ye be vexed with, this medicine shall surely make you whole, as men say.

" *The Office of Usher and Marshal*

" An usher or marshal, without fail, must know all the estates of the Church, and the excellent estate of a king with his honourable blood. This is a notable nurture, cunning, curious and commendable.

" The estate of the Pope has no peer, an emperor is next him everywhere and a King is correspondent, a high cardinal next in dignity, then a King's son (ye call him prince), an archbishop his equal; a duke of the blood royal; a bishop, marquis and earl coequal; a viscount, legate, baron, suffragan and mitred abbot; a baron of the exchequer, the three chief justices and the Mayor of London; a cathedral prior, unmitred

abbot and knight bachelor ; a prior, dean, archdeacon,
knight and body esquire ; the Master of the Rolls (as
I reckon aright), and puisne judge ; clerk of the crown
and the exchequer, and you may pleasantly prefer the
Mayor of Calais.[1]

" A provincial,[2] doctor of divinity and prothonotary [3]
may dine together ; and you may place the pope's
legate or collector with a doctor of both laws.   An ex-
mayor of London ranks with a serjeant-at-law, next a
Mastery of Chancery, and then a worshipful preacher
of pardons,[4] masters of arts, and religious orders,
parsons and vicars, and parish priests with a cure, the
bailiffs of a city, a yeoman of the crown, and serjeant-
of-arms with his mace, with him a herald, the King's
herald in the first place, worshipful merchants and
rich artificers, gentlemen well-nurtured and of good
manners, together with gentlewomen and lords' foster-
mothers [5]—all these may eat with squires.

" Lo, son, I have now told you, after my simple wit,

---

[1] See note.   [2] Head of a monastic order for a province.
[3] Chief clerk (ecclesiastical office).
[4] Compare Chaucer's Pardoner in his *Prologue.*
[5] *Nurrieris :* Latin, *nutricarii* ?

the rank of every estate according to his degree, and
now I will show you how they should be grouped at
table in respect of their dignity, and how they should
be served.

"The pope, an emperor, king, cardinal, prince with
a golden royal rod,[1] archbishop in his pall—all these
for their dignity ought not to dine in the hall.

"A bishop, viscount, marquis, goodly earl may sit
at two messes if they be agreeable thereunto.

"The Mayor of London, a baron, a mitred abbot,
the three chief justices, the Speaker of Parliament—all
these estates are great and honourable, and they may
sit together in chamber or hall, two or three at a mess,
if it so please them ; but in your office you must try
to please every man.

"The other estates, three or four to a mess, equal
to a knight's, are : unmitred abbot or prior, dean,
archdeacon, Master of the Rolls, all the under judges
and barons of the king's exchequer, a provincial, a
doctor of divinity or of both laws, a prothonotary, or
the pope's collector, if he be there, and the Mayor of
the Staple.

[1] Sceptre.   See note.

"Other ranks you may set four to a mess, of persons equal to a squire in dignity, serjeants-at-law and ex-mayors of London, the masters of Chancery, all preachers, residencers, and parsons, apprentices of the law, merchants and franklins—these may sit properly at a squire's table.

"Each estate shall sit at meat by itself, not seeing the others, at meal-time or in the field or in the town; and each must sit alone in the chamber or in the pavilion.

"The Bishop of Canterbury shall be served apart from the Archbishop of York, and the Metropolitan shall be served alone. The Bishop of York must not be served in the presence of the Primate of England.[1]

"Now, son, from divers causes, as equally from ignorance, a marshal is often puzzled how to rank lords of royal blood who are poor, and others not of royal blood who are rich, also ladies of royal blood wedded to knights, and poor ladies marrying those of royal blood. The lady of royal blood shall keep her rank, the lady of low blood and degree shall take her husband's rank. The substance of livelihood[2] is not so

[1] See note.   [2] Property, wealth.

digne[1] as royal blood, wherefore this prevails in chamber and hall, for some day blood royal might attain to the kingship.

" If the parents of a pope or cardinal be still alive, they must in no wise presume to be equal to their son, either sitting or standing. The estate of their son will not allow them either to sit or stand by him—nor should they desire it; wherefore they should have a separate chamber assigned to them.

" A marshal must look to the birth of each estate, and arrange officers such as chancellor, steward, chamberlain, treasurer, according to their degree.

" He must honour foreign visitors, and strangers to this land, even when they are resident here. A well-trained marshal should think beforehand how to place strangers at the table, for if they show gentle cheer and good manners, he thereby doth honour his lord and bring praise to himself.

" If the king send any messenger to your lord, if he be a knight, squire, yeoman of the crown, groom, page or child, receive him honourably as a baron, knight, squire, yeoman or groom,[2] and so forth, from the

[1] Worthy of reverence.   [2] See note.

highest degree to the lowest, for a king's groom may
dine with a knight or a marshal.

"A commendable marshal must also understand the
rank of all the worshipful officers of the commonalty of
this land, of shires, cities and boroughs—such must be
placed in due order, according to their rank.

"The estate of a knight of [good] blood and wealth
is not the same as that of a simple and poor knight.
Also, the Mayor of Queenborough [1] is not of like
dignity with the Mayor of London—nothing like of
degree ; and they must on no account sit at the same
table.

"The Abbot of Westminster is the highest in the
land, and the Abbot of Tintern the poorest ; both are
abbots, yet Tintern shall neither sit nor stand with
Westminster.[1] Also, the Prior of Dudley may in no
wise sit with the Prior of Canterbury.[1] And remember, as a general rule, that a prior who is a prelate
of a cathedral church, shall sit above any abbot or prior
of his own diocese, in church, chapel, chamber or hall.

"Reverend doctors of twelve years' standing shall
sit above those of nine years', although the latter may

[1] See note.

spend more largely of fine red gold. Likewise, the younger aldermen shall sit or stand below their elders, and so in every craft, the master first, and then the ex-warden.

" All these points, with many more, belong to the duty of a marshal; and so before every feast think what estates shall sit in the hall, and reason with yourself before your lord shall call upon you. If you are in any doubt, go either to your lord or to the chief officer, and then shall you do no wrong or prejudice to any state; but set all according to their birth, riches or dignity.

" Now, good son, I have shown you the courtesy of the court, and how to manage in pantry, buttery, cellar or in carving, as a sewer or as a marshal. I suppose ye be sure in these sciences, which in my day I learned with a royal prince, to whom I was usher and also marshal.

" All the officers I have mentioned have to obey me, ever to fulfil my commandment when I call, for our office is the chief in spicery and cellar, whether the cook be lief or loth.[1]

[1] See note.

" All these divers offices may be filled by a single person, but the dignity of a prince requireth each office to have its officer and a servant waiting on him. Moreover, all must know their duties perfectly, for doubt and fear are a hindrance in serving a lord and pleasing his guests.

" Fear not to serve a prince—God be his speed! Take good heed to your duties, and be ever on the watch, and thus doing as ye should, there will be no need to doubt.

" Tasting is done only for those of royal blood, as pope, emperor, empress, cardinal, king, queen, prince, archbishop, duke or earl—none other that I call to remembrance. It is done for fear of poison, so let each man in office keep his room secure and close his safe,[1] chest and storehouse for fear of conspiracy.

" The steward and chamberlain of a prince of the blood must know about homages, services and fewte ; [2] and as they have the oversight of all other offices and of the tasting, they must tell the marshal, sewer or carver, how to do it ; and he must be in no fear when he tasteth.

" As the evening draws in, and I cannot tarry, I do

[1] Text, *gardevyan ;* Fr. *gardeviande.*   [2] Fealty.

not propose to contrive more of this matter. This treatise that I have entitled, if ye would prove it, I myself assayed in youth, when I was young and lusty; and I enjoyed these aforesaid matters, and took good heed to learn. But crooked age hath now compelled me to leave the court, so assay for yourself, my son, and God speed you!"

"Now, fair befall you, father, and blessings be on you for thus teaching me! I shall dare to do diligent service to divers dignitaries, where before I was afraid for the scantiness of my knowledge; I perceive the whole matter so perfectly that I am ready to try my part, and some good I may learn from practice and exercise. I am bound always to pray God reward you for your gentle teaching of me!"

"Now, good son, thyself and others that shall succeed thee to note, learn and read over this book of nurture, pray for the soul of John Russell, servant to Humphrey, Duke of Gloucester. Pray for that peerless prince, and for the souls of my wife and my father and mother, unto Mary, Mother and Maid, that she defend us from our foes, and bring us all to bliss when we go hence. Amen."

[The *envoi* may have been added later [1]]

" Go forth, little book, and lowly thou me commend,
Unto all young gentlemen that list to learn or entend,[2]
And specially to them that have experience, praying
    them to amend,
And correct what is amiss, whereas I fail or offend.
And if so that any be found as through my negligence,
Cast the cause on my copy, rude and bare of eloquence,
Which to draw out [I] have done my busy diligence,
Readily to reform it by reason and better sentence.

As for rhyme or reason, the fore-writer was not to
    blame,
For as he found it before him, so wrote he the same,
And though he or I in our matter digress or degrade,
Blame neither of us, for we never it made ;
Simple, as I had insight, somewhat the rhyme I correct.
Blame I could no man, I have no person suspect.
Now, good God, grant us grace our souls never to infect,
Then we may reign in thy region eternally with thine
    elect."

       [1] See note.   [2] Hear.

THE BOOK OF COURTESY

Here beginneth the First Book of Courtesy

WHOSO will of courtesy hear,
    In this book it is made clear.
If thou be gentleman, yeoman or knave,
Thee needeth nurture for to have.
When thou comest to a lord's gate,
The porter thou shalt find thereat;
Take [1] him thou shalt thy weapon to,
And ask him leave in to go,
To speak with lord, lady, squire or groom,
Thereof thou must bethink thee soon;
For if he be of low degree,
Then him falls to come to thee.
If he be gentleman of kin
The porter thee will lead to him.
When thou comest the hall door to,
Take off thy hood, thy gloves off do.
If the hall at the first meat be,
Forget not this lesson concerns thee:
The steward, controller and treasurer there,
Sitting at the daïs, hail thou fair.

[1] Give.

Within the hall set on either side,
Sit other gentlemen, as falls that tide.
Incline thee fair to them also,
First to the right hand thou shalt go,
Sithen [1] to the left hand thine eye thou cast,
To them thou bowest full fast.
Take heed to yeomen on thy right hand,
And sithen before the screen thou stand,
Amid the hall upon the floor,
While marshal or usher come fro the door,
And bid thee sit or to board thee lead.
Be stable of cheer for manners, take heed.
If ye be set at a gentleman's board,
Look thou be hend [2] and little of word.
Pare thy bread and carve in two
The overcrust from the nether through.
In four thou cut the overdole,[3]
Set them together as it were whole,
After, cut the nether crust in three,
And turn it down—learn this of me.
And set thy trencher thee before,
And sit upright for any sore.

[1] Afterwards.   [2] Courteous.   [3] Upper deal, *i.e.*, part.

Spare bread or wine, drink or ale,
Till thy mess from the kitchen be set in hall,
Lest men say thou art hunger-beaten,
Or all men know thee for a glutton.
Look thy nails be clean, in truth,
Lest thy fellow loathe them, forsooth.
Bite not thy bread and lay it down,
That is no courtesy to use in town.
As much as thou wilt eat, that break,
The remnant left the poor shall take.
In peace thou eat and ever eschew
To quarrel at board—that may thee rue.
If thou make mows in any wise
A villainy thou catchest or ever thou rise,
Let never thy cheek be great with meat,
Or morsel of bread that thou shalt eat.
An ape's mow men say he makes
That bread and flesh in his cheek bakes.[1]
If any man speak that time to thee,
And thou shalt answer, it will not be
But wallowing,[1] and thou must abide ;
That is a shame for all beside.

[1] See note.

On both sides of thy mouth if thou eat,
Many a scorning shalt thou get.
Thou shalt not laugh nor speak nothing,
While thy mouth be full of meat or drink.
Nor sup thou not with great sounding,
Neither pottage, nor other thing.
Let not thy spoon stand in thy dish,
Whether thou be served with flesh or fish,
Nor lay it not on thy dish side,
But cleanse it honestly without pride.
Look that no dirt on thy finger be,
To defoul the cloth before thee.
In thy dish if thou wet thy bread,
Look thereof that nought be led
To drip again thy dish into ;
Thou art ill-bred if thou so do.
Dry thy mouth ay well and fine,
Whether thou shalt drink ale or wine,
Nor call thou not a dish again
That is taken from the board in plain.[1]
If thou spit over the board or else on't,
Thou shalt be holden courtesy to want.

[1] Altogether.

If thine own dog thou scrape or claw
For a vice that is held as men know.
If thy nose thou cleanse, as may befall,
Look thy hand thou cleanse withal ;
Privily with skirt do it away,
Or else thro' thy tippet that is so gay.
At meat cleanse not thy teeth nor pick
With knife or straw or wand or stick.
While thou holdest meat in mouth, beware
To drink, that is an unhonest chare ; [1]
And also physic forbids it quite,
And says thou may be choked at that bite,
If it go wrong thy throat into
And stop thy wind, thou art fordo. [2]
Nor tell thou never at board no tale
To harm or shame thy fellow in hall ;
For if he then withhold his wrath,
Eftsoons he will forecast thy death.
Wheresoever thou sit at meat by the board,
Avoid [3] the cat, at a bare word ;
For if thou stroke or cat or dog,
Thou art like an ape tied with a clog.

[1] Trick or turn. See note.   [2] Done for.   [3] Turn out ?

Also eschew, without strife,
To foul the board-cloth [1] with thy knife.
Nor blow not on thy drink or meat,
Neither for cold, neither for heat.
Nor bear with meat thy knife to mouth,
Whether thou be set by strong or couth.[2]
Nor with no board-cloth thy teeth thou clean
Nor eyen that run red, as may be seen.
If thou sit by a right good man
This lesson look thou think upon :
Under his thigh put not thy knee
Thou art full lewd if thou let this be.
Nor backward sitting give thou thy cup
Neither to drink, neither to sup.
Bid thy friend take cup and drink,
That is holden an honest thing.
Lean not on elbow at thy meat,
Neither for cold nor for heat.
Dip not thy thumb thy drink into ;
Thou art uncourteous if thou it do.
In salt-cellar if thou put
Or fish or flesh that men see it,

[1] Table-cloth.   [2] Polite.

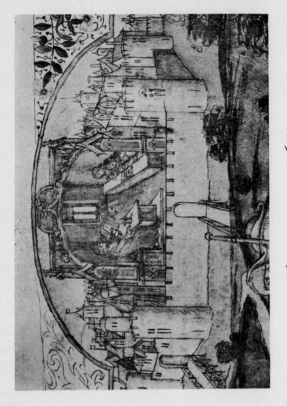

"If there be a young Infant"

That is a vice, as men me tells;
And great wonder it would be else.
After meat when thou shalt wash,
Spit not in basin nor water dash,
Nor spit not loosely for any meed
Before a man of God for dread.
Whosoever despises this lesson right
At board to sit he has no might.
Here endeth now our first talking.
Christ grant us all his dear blessing!

Here endeth the First Book of Courtesy

THE SECOND BOOK

If thou be a young infant
And think the schools for to haunt,
This lesson shall thy master thee mark—
Cross-Christ [1] thee speed in all thy work.
After [2] thy *Pater Noster* he will thee teach,
As Christ's own apostles did preach;
After, thy *Ave Maria* and thy *Creed*,
That shall thee save at doom of dread.

[1] See note.   [2] [First]?

Then after to bless thee with the Trinity,
In nomine patris he will teach thee.
Then with Mark, Matthew, Luke and John
With thee *Per crucis* and the high name,
To shrive thee in general thou shalt learn
Thy *Confiteor* and *Misereatur* in turn.
To seek the kingdom of God, my child,
Thereto I rede thou be not wild ;
But worship God, both old and young,
To be in body and soul alike strong.
When thou comest to the church door,
Take the holy water standing on floor.
Read or sing or bid prayers
To Christ, for all thy Christian confreres.
Be courteous to God and kneel adown
On both knees [1] with great devotion.
To man thou shalt kneel upon the one
The t'other [2] to thy self thou hold alone.
When thou ministers at the high altar [see]
With both hands thou serve the priest [reverently],
The one to stable the t'other
Lest thou fail, my dear brother.

[1] See note.   [2] So in text.

Another courtesy I will thee teach :
Thy father and mother with mild speech
To worship and serve with all thy might,
That thou dwell the longer in earthly light.
To another man, do no more amiss
Than thou would'st be done of him and his ;
So Christ thou pleases and gets thee love
Of men, and God that sits above.
Be not too meek, but in mean thou hold,
For else a fool thou wilt be told.
He that to righteousness will incline,
As Holy Writ tells us, well and fine,
Never go seek their bread shall his seed,
Nor suffer of man no shameful deed.
To forgive thou shalt thee haste,
To vengeance look thou come at last.[1]
Draw thee to peace with all thy strength,
From strife and debate draw thee at length.
If a man ask thee goods for God's sake,
And thee want things whereof to take,
Give him debonaire words and manner fair,
With semblance glad, and pure good cheer.

[1] Last of all.

Also of service thou shalt be free
To every man in his degree,
That one shall never lose for to be kind ;
He who forgets one, has another in mind.
If a man have part with thee in gift,
With him thou make an even shift.[1]
Let it not hang in hand for glose ; [2]
Thou art uncourteous if thou it does.
To saints [3] if thou thy gate [4] hast hight [5]
Thou shalt fulfil it with all thy might,
Lest God thee strike with great vengeánce,
And put thee into sore penánce.
Believe not all men that speak thee fair,
Whether they be commons, burgess or mayor ;
In sweet words the adder was closed,[6]
Deceiving ever and mysloset.[7]
Therefore thou art of Adam's blood,
Of words beware lest thou be wode.[8]
A short word is commonly sooth,
That first slides from a man's tooth.

[1] Share.   [2] Flattery.   [3] On a pilgrimage.
[4] Way.   [5] Promised.   [6] Enclosed.   See note.
[7] Misleading (?)   See note.   [8] Mad.

Look liar that thou never become :
Keep this word for all and some.
Laugh not too oft for no soláce,
Never for mirth that any man has.[1]
Who laughs that all men may him see,
A shrew [2] or a fool him seems to be.
Three enemies in this world there are,
That covet all men to forfare : [3]
The devil, the flesh, the world also,
That work mankind full mickle woe.
If thou may destroy these enemies three
Thou may secure of Heaven's bliss be.
Also, my children, against thy lord
Look thou strive with no manner word,
Nor wager none with him thou lay,
Nor at the dice with him do play.
Him that thou knows of greater state
Be not his fellow in rest or debate.[4]
If thou be bestead [5] in strange countrée,
Search out no further than falls to thee ;
Nor take no more to do in hand,

[1] See note.   [2] Wicked man.   [3] Destroy.
[4] Strife.   [5] In straits.

Than thou may have worship of all in land.
If thou see any man fall in the street,
Laugh not thereat in dry nor wet ;
But help him up with all thy might,
As St. Ambrose [1] thee teaches right.
Thou that stands so sure on seat,
'Ware lest thy head fall to thy feet.
My child, if thou be at the Mass,
That understand both more and less,[1]
If the priest read not at thy will,
Reprove him not but hold thee still.
To any wight if counsel thou shew,
Beware that he be not a shrew,
Lest he slander thee with tongue,
Among all men, both old and young.
Beckoning, fingering, none thou use ;
And privy whispering look thou refuse.
If thou meet knight, yeoman or knave,
Hail him anon, " Sir, God you save,"
If he speak first upon thee there,
Answer him gladly without demur.
Go not forth as a dumb freak,[2]

[1] See note.   [2] Fellow.

Since God has given thee tongue to speak,
Lest men say to friend or gossip :
" Yonder is a man ne'er opens his lip." [1]
Speak never wrong of womenkind,
Nor let it never run in thy mind.
The book him calls of churlish face
That oft of women speaks villainy base.
For all we be of women born,
And our fathers us beforn ;
Therefore it is an unhonest thing
To do them any belittling.[2]
Also to a wife befalls of right
To worship her husband both day and night ;
To his bidding to show obediénce,
And him to serve without offence.
If two brethren be in debate
Look neither thou further in their hate ;
But help to staunch [3] them of uncharity ;
Then thou art friend of both certainly.
If thou go with another at the gate,
And ye be both of one estate,
Be courteous and let him have the way :

[1] See note.   [2] Text: *hethyng*, scorn.   [3] Stop. See note.

That is no villainy, as men me say.
If he be come of great kindred,
Go not before though thou be bid ;
And if that he thy master be,
Go not before for courtesy,
Neither in field, wood nor lawnd,[1]
Nor even [2] with him, unless he command.
If thou shalt on pilgrimage go,
Be not third fellow, for weal nor woe ;
Three oxen [3] in plough may never well draw,
Neither by craft, right, nor law.
If thou be proffered to drink of cup
Drink not all off, nor no way sup ;
Drink mannerly [4] and give again :
That is a courtesy, to speak in plain.
In bed if thou fall harboured to be
With fellow, master, or their degree,
Thou shalt inquire by courtesy,
In what part of the bed he will lie.
Be honest and lie thou far him fro ;

---

[1] Glade.   [2] Side by side.   [3] See note.
[4] Text: *menskly*, *i.e.*, in its original sense, like a human
being.

Thou art not wise but thou do so.
With whatso man, both far and nigh,
Thee falls to go, look thou be sly [1]
To ask his name, and which he be,
Whither he will : keep well these three.
With friars on pilgrimage if that thou go
What they will observe, will thou also.
When at night thou take thy rest,
And bide the day as true man's guest,
In never house where a red man [1] be,
Nor woman of the same colour certainly,
Take never thine inn for no manner need,
For those be folk to hold in dread.
If any in sternness thee oppose,
Answer him meekly, and make him glose ; [2]
But glosing word that falséd [3] is
Forsake, and all that is amiss.
Also, if thou have a lord,
And stand before him at the board,
While that thou speak, keep well thy hand ;
Thy foot also in peace let stand.
His courtesy needs must he break,

[1] See note.   [2] Fair words.   [3] Falsified.

Stirring fingers or toes whene'er he shall speak.[1]
Be stable of cheer and somewhat light,
Nor over all wave [2] thou not thy sight.
Gaze not on walls with thine eye,
Far nor near, low nor high.
Let not the post become thy staff,
Lest thou be called a " doted daff." [3]
Nor delve thou never thy nostril,
With thumb or finger as young girl.
Rub not thy arm, nor claw it naught,
Nor bow thy head too low in aught.
While any man speaks with great businéss,
Hearken his words without distress.
By street or way if thou shalt go,
From these two things thou keep thee fro ;
Neither to harm child nor beast,
With casting, turning west nor east.
Nor change thou not in face colour,
For lightness of word in hall or bower ;
If thy visage change for nought,
Men say thee : " Trespass thou hast wrought."
Before thy lord no mows thou make,

[1] See note.   [2] Cast about.   [3] Silly fool.

If thou wilt courtesy with thee take.

With hands unwashen take never thy meat :

From all these vices look thou keep.

Look thou sit—and make no strife—

Where the host commands, or else his wife.

Eschew the highest place to win,[1]

Save thou be bidden to sit therein.

Of courtesy here ends the second fit.[2]

To heaven Christ grant our souls to flit !

THE THIRD BOOK

De Officiariis in Curiis Dominorum [3]

Now of officers speak will we,

Of court, and also of their duty.[4]

Four men there be that yards shall bear :

Porter, marshal, steward, ushér.

The porter shall have the longest wand,

The marshal a shorter shall have in hand ;

---

[1] Fight for. Text: *with win*, which may mean " with pleasure."

[2] A section of a poem, commonly of a ballad.

[3] *Of the Officers in Lords' Halls.*   [4] Fr. *mestiers.*

The usher of chamber smallest shall have,
The steward in hand shall have a staff
A finger great,[1] two quarters [2] long,
  To rule the men of court among.

De Janitore [3]

The porter falls to keep the gate,
The stocks [4] with him, early and late
If any man has in court misgone,
To-porter-ward he shall be tane,
There to abide the lord's will,
What he will deem [4] by righteous skill.
For " wesselle clothes " [4] that be not sold,
The porter has that ward in hold.
Of strangers, also, that come in court,
The porter shall warn, sir, at a word.
He is found in meat and drink,
And sits with him [4] whoso him think.
Whensoever the lord remove shall,
One castle til t'other, as it may fall,
For carriage the porter horses shall hire,

[1] Thick.   [2] Of a yard or ell.   [3] *Of the Porter.*   [4] See note.

Four pence a-piece [1] within the shire,
By statute he shall take [1] on that day :
That is the king's cry,[2] i' fay.

De Marescallo Aule [3]

Now of marshal of hall will I spell,
And what falls to his office now will I tell.
In absence of steward, he shall arrest
Whomsoever is rebel in court or feast.
Yeoman-usher and groom also—
Under him are these two.
The groom brings fuel that shall bren,[4]
In hall, chamber and kitchen, I ken.
He shall deliver it every deal,
In hall make fire at each meal.
Board, trestles and forms also,
The cupboard [1] in his ward shall go.
The canopies, curtains to hang in hall—
These offices needs do he shall.
Bring in fire on All Hallows' Day,
To Candlemas Even,[5] I dare well say.

[1] See note.   [2] Proclamation.
[3] *Of the Marshal of the Hall.*   [4] Burn.   [5] February 2nd.

*Per quantum Tempus Armigeri habebunt Liberatam
et Ignis Ardebit in Aula* [1]

So long squires liveries [2] shall have,
Of groom of hall, or else his knave.
But fire shall burn in hall at meat
Until *Cena Domini* [3] men have eat.
There brought shall be a holly keen,[2]
That set shall be in arbour green ;
And that shall be till All Hallows' Day,
And off be shifted, as I you say.
In hall marshal all men shall set
After their degree, without let.

De Pincernario, Panetario, et Cocis sibi Servientibus [4]

The butler, panter and cooks also
To him are servants without mo.[5]

---

[1] *For how long Squires shall have Liveries, and Fire Burn
in Hall.*
[2] See note.
[3] Shere-Thursday, *i.e.* Thursday before Easter.
[4] *Of the Butler, Panter and Cooks as Servants to him* (the
marshal).
[5] More.

Therefore on his yard score [1] shall he,
All messes in hall that served shall be,
Command to set both bread and ale
To all men that served be in hall.
To gentlemen with heated drink,
Else fails the service, as I think.
Each mess at six pence [1] booked shall be
At the counting-house, with other meiny.
If the cook would say that there were more,
That is the cause he has it in score; [1]
The panter also if he would strive
For reward that set shall be belive.[2]
When bread fails at board about,
The marshal gars set, without a doubt,
More bread that called is a reward,
So shall it be proved before steward.

De Officio Pincernarii [3]

Butler shall set for each mess
A pot, a loaf, without distress.[4]
Butler, panter, fellows are aye;

[1] See note.
[2] Quickly.
[3] Of the Butler's Office.
[4] Without being compelled.

Reckon them together full well I may.
The marshal shall harbour all men in [ward] [1]
That be of any office at court,
Save the lord's chamber, the wardrobe too,
The usher of chamber shall heed [2] those two.

De Hostiario et suis Servientibus [3]

Speak I will a little while
Of usher of chamber without guile.
There is gentleman-, yeoman-usher [4] also,
Two grooms at the least, a page thereto.

De Officio Garcionum [5]

Grooms shall make litter [4] and stuff pallets out,
Nine foot in length without a doubt,
Seven foot certainly shall it be broad,
Well watered and bound together, craftily trod,
With wisps drawn out at feet and side,
Well twisted and turned again, that tide.
Unsunken in hollows shall it be made,

---

[1] Text: *in fine*, *i.e.* together. See note.
[2] Text: *tent* (Scotch).   [3] *Of the Usher and his Servants.*
[4] See note.   [5] *Of the Grooms' Office.*

Both outer and inner, so God me glad.

That shall be hung with a canopy hollow,

And hooks and loops on bands shall follow.

The valance on a rod shall hang with state,[1]

Three curtains drawn within full straight,

That reach shall even to ground about,

Neither more, neither less, without a doubt.

He strikes them up with a forkéd wand,

And laps[2] up fast about the left hand,

The button[3] up turns and closes on the right,

As a man by the neck that hangs full light.[4]

The counterpane he lays on the bed's feet,

Cushions on the side shall lie full meet.

Carpets of Spain on the floor beside,

That spread should be for pomp and pride.

The chamber sides right to the door,

He hangs with tapestries[5] full store.[6]

And fuel to chimney him falls to get

And screens in cloth[7] to save the heat,

---

[1] Text: *wyn*, joy.   [2] Wraps or fastens

[3] Text: *knop*.   [4] See note.

[5] *tapets*—(1) carpets, (2) hangings.

[6] Scandinavian, *stor*, great.

[7] Text: *clof*, Dr. Furnivall conjectures "cloth."

From the lord at meat when he is set.
Boards, trestles and forms, without let,
All these things keep shall he there,
And water in chafer [1] for ladies fair.
Three perchers [2] of wax then shall he get,
Above the chimney that be set,
In socket each one from other shall be
The length of that other, that men may see
To burn, to avoid what drunken is ;
Or else, I wot, he does amiss.
The usher alway shall sit at door
At meat, and walk shall on the floor,
To see that all be served aright—
That is his office, both day and night.
And bid set board when time shall be,
And take them [3] up when time sees he.
The wardrobe he harbours eke of chamber—
Ladies with beads of coral and amber.
The usher shall bid the wardrober
Make ready for all night before the fire.
Then brings he forth nightgown also,

[1] Heater.   [2] Big candles, Paris candles.
[3] The board and trestles.   See note.

And spreads a carpet and cushions two.

He lays them then upon a form

And foot-sheet thereon, and it doth return,[1]

The lord shall shift his gown at night,

Sitting on foot-sheet till he be dight.

Then usher goes to the buttery,

" Have in for all night, sir," says he.

First to the chandler he shall go

To take a night-light [2] him fro ;

Both wine and ale he takes indeed.

The butler says without dread :

" No meat for man assayed shall be

But for king or prince or duke so free.

For Heirs-Apparent also it is,

Meat shall be assayed, now think on this."

Then to the pantry he hies belive :

" Sirs, have in, without strife."

Fine bread [3] and common bread [4] he shall take ;

The panter assays that it be bake.

A mortar [5] of wax yet will he bring

[1] Turn back, or fold.   [2] Text: *tortes*, *i.e.* taper.
[3] Manchet, white bread.   [4] Cheat-bread, of whole meal.
[5] A cake or lump, perhaps shaped especially to serve as
a night-light.

For chamber, sir, without lying,
That all night burns in a basin clear
To save the chamber at night from fire.
Then yeoman of chamber shall void the rime [1]
The torches have holden well that time.
The chamber door stekes [2] the usher then
With pricket [3] and candle that can bren.
From cupboard he brings both bread and wine,
And first assays it, well and fine.
But first the lord shall wash, i' fay,
When he comes from the further house away.
Then kneels the usher and gives him drink,
Brings him in bed where he shall wink.
In strong stead on pallet he lay, [4]
Of them takes leave and goes his way.
Yeoman-usher before the door,
In outer chamber, lies on the floor.

[1] Probably, crust of soot.
[2] Scotch, fastens, secures.
[3] A spike on which a candle was thrust instead of being placed in a socket.
[4] See note.

De Seneschallo [1]

Now will I speak of the steward too ;—
Many are false, but few are [true [2]].
The clerk of kitchen; controller,
Steward, cook, and surveyor,
Assent in council without scorn
How the lord shall fare at meat the morn.
If any dainty in country be,
The steward shows it to the lord so free,
Bids to buy it for any cost—
It were great sin if it were lost.
Before the course the steward comes then,
The server it next, of all kinds of men,
Makes way and stands beside,
Till all be served at that tide.
At counting steward shall be seen
Till all be booked in wax so green,[2]
Written into books without let,
That before in tables has been set,
Till accounts also thereon be cast,
And summed up wholly at the last.

[1] *Of the Steward.*   [2] See note.

De Contrarotulatore [1]

The controller shall write to him,
" *Taunt resceu* " [2]—no more, I mean ;
And " *Taunt dispendu* " [3] that same day ;
Uncountable [4] he is, as I you say.

De Supervisore [5]

Surveyor and steward also,
These three folk and no mo
For nought receive, but ever see
That nothing fail and all things agree.
That the clerk of kitchen should not miss—
Therefore the controller, as have I bliss,
Writes up the sum as every day,
And helps to count as I you say.

De Clerico Coquine [6]

The clerk of kitchen shall all things brief, [7]
Of men of court, both loth and lief ;

[1] *Of the Controller.*   [2] So much received.
[3] So much spent.
[4] Unaccountable, *i.e.* not responsible to a higher officer (?)
[5] *Of the Surveyor.*   See note.
[6] *Of the Clerk of the Kitchen.*   [7] Book.

Of purchases and dispenses then writes he
And wages for grooms and yeomen free.
At dresser also he shall stand,
And fetch forth meat dressed by hand.
The spicery and stores with him shall dwell,
And many things else, as I nought tell,
For clothing of every officer,
Save the lord himself and ladies dear.

De Cancellario [1]

The chancellor answers for their clothing,
For yeomen, falconers, and their horsing,
For their wardrobe and wages also,
And seals patents, many and mo.
If the lord give all for term of life,
The chancellor it seals without strife.
" *Tan come nos plerra,*" men say, that is, " *Quando
    placet nobis,*"
That is, while us likes, be nought amiss.
Oversees his lands that all be right ;
One of the great he is of might.

[1] *Of the Chancellor.*

De Thesaurizario [1]

Now to speak of the treasurer I come.
Husband and housewife he is in one.
Of the receiver he shall receive
All that is gathered of bailiff and reeve,
Of the lord's courts, and forfeits [2] too,
Whether they be false or they be true.
To the clerk of the kitchen he pays money
For victual to buy throughout the country.
The clerk to caterer and poulterer is,
To baker and butler both, so 'tis,
Gives silver to buy in all thing,
What belongs to their office without lying.
The treasurer shall give all kinds of wage
To squire, yeoman, groom or page.
The receiver and the treasurer,
The clerk of kitchen and chancellor,
Reeves and bailiffs and parker, [3]
Shall come to accounts every year,
Before the auditor of the lord anon,
That shall be true as any stone.

[1] *Of the Treasurer.*   [2] Fines.   [3] Park-keeper.

If he treats them not right leal
To a baron of exchequer they must appeal.

De Receptore Firmarum [1]

Of the receiver speak will I
That farms [2] receiveth, verily,
Of reeves and them a quittance [3] makes ;
Six pence thereof as fee he takes.
And pays fees to parks as I know ;
Therefore at accounts he loved is so.
And oversees castles and manors about,
That naught fall, within or without.
Now let we these officers be,
And of smaller folk tell we.

De Avenario [4]

The avener shall provender wisely ordain,
All the lord's horses to maintain.
They shall have two cast [5] of hay,
A peck of provender in a day.

---

[1] *Of the Receiver of Rents.*   [2] Rents.   [3] Receipt.
[4] *Of the Avener.*   The office is explained.
[5] As much as a pitchfork could cast.

Every horse shall so much have,
At rack and manger that stands with staff.[1]
There is a master of horses, a squire,
Under him avener and farrier.
These yeomen old saddles shall have
That shall be last for knight and knave.
For each horse a farrier shall shoe,
A ha'penny a day he takes him to.
Under be grooms and pages many a one,
That be at wages every one,
Some at twopence by the day,
And some at three farthings, I you say.
Many of them footmen there been
That run by the bridles of ladies sheen.

De Pistore [2]

Of the baker now speak I will,
And what belongs his office till.
Of a London bushel he shall bake
Twenty loaves I undertake :
Manchet [3] and cheat,[4] to make brown bread hard
For chandler and greyhound and hunt reward.

---

[1] Bar before the hayrack.
[2] *Of the Baker.*
[3] Bread of finely sifted flour.
[4] Wholemeal bread.

De Venatore et suis Canibus [1]

A ha'penny the hunt takes on the day,
For every hound, the sooth to say.
Two cast [2] of bread has the fewterer,[3]
If two leash of greyhounds there are,
To each a bone, that is to tell,
If I the sooth to you shall spell,
Besides his vantage [4] that may befall
Of skins and other things withal.
That hunters better can tell than I,
And therefore I leave it utterly.

De Aquario [5]

And speak I will of other gear
That falls to court, as ye may hear.
An ewerer in hall there needs to be,
And candles shall have and all napery.
He shall give water to gentlemen,
And also to all yeomen,

[1] *Of the Huntsman and his Dogs.*
[2] Handfuls, lit., throws.
[3] Keeper of greyhounds.   [4] **Profit in kind.**
[5] *Of the Ewerer.*

" *Qui debent manus lavare et in quorum domibus,*" [1]

In king's court and duke's also,

There yeomen shall wash and no mo.

In Duke John's [2] house a yeoman there was

For his reward prayed such a grace.

The duke got grant thereof in land

Of the king, his father, I understand.

Whosoever gives water in king's chamber,

In presence of lord or lady dear,

He shall kneel down upon his knee,

Else he forgets his courtesy.

This ewerer shall cover his lord's board

With double napery, at a bare word,

The selvage toward the lord's side ;

And down shall hang that other wide. [2]

The uppercloth shall double be laid,

To the outer side the selvage braid ; [3]

The other selvage he shall over fold

As towel it were, fair to behold.

Napkins he shall cast thereupon,

That the lord shall cleanse his fingers on ;

---

[1] " *Who ought to wash hands, and in whose houses.*"
[2] See note.   [3] Scotch, for *broad.*

John of Gaunt receives a civic deputation.

The lady and whosoever sits in hall,
All napkins shall have, both great and small.

De Panetario [1]

Then comes the panter with loaves three,
That square are carven for trencher free,
Two set within and one without,
And salt-cellar covered and set *en route ;* [2]
With the overmost loaf it shall be set,
To make up the square, without let.
Two carving knives are placéd soon,
The third to the lord, and also a spoon.

De Cultellis Domini [3]

Of the two the hafts shall outward be,
Of the third the haft inward lays he.
The spoon handle shall be laid thereby,
More trenchers and loaves there full nigh
He sets, and ever must he bear
To duchess his wine that is so dear.

[1] *Of the Panter.*   [2] In its place.
              [3] *Concerning the Lord's Knives.*

Two loaves of trenchers and salt too,
He sets before his son also.
A loaf of trenchers and salt at last
At board's end he sets in haste.
Then bread he brings in towel wrapped aright;
Three loaves shall be given of the white,
A cheat-loaf [1] to the alms-dish,
Whether he served be with flesh or fish.
At either end he casts a cope,[2]
Laid down on board, the ends turned up.
That he assays kneeling on knee—
The carver him pares a slice [3] so free—
And touches the loaves in a circle [4] about;
The panter it eats without a doubt.
The ewerer through towels straineth clean
His water into the basins sheen.
The over-basin thereon shall close,
A towel thereon, as I suppose,
That folded shall be with full great lore,
Two quarters in length and somewhat more.
A white cup of wood thereby shall be,

---

[1] Wholemeal loaf.   [2] Covering, towel.
[3] Text: *shiver*, i.e., sliver.   [4] Text: *quere.*

Therewith with water assay shall he,
Covers it again before all men.
The carver the basins takes up then,
The announcing squire or else a knight,
The towel down takes by full good right;
The cup he takes in hand also,
The carver pours water the cup into.
The knight the carver holds anon to,
He assays it ere he more shall do.
The cup then voided is in hall away;
The ewerer takes it without delay.
The towel two knights together shall bear,
Before the lord's sleeves that be so dear.
The over-basin they hold, never the whether,[1]
While the carver pours water into the nether;
For a pipe there is inside so clean,
That water devoids,[2] of silver sheen.
Then sets he the nether, I understand,
In the over and voids with either hand,
And brings to the ewerer where he came fro.
To the lord's boards again doth go,
And lays four trenchers the lord before,

[1] None the less.   [2] Empties.

The fifth above, by good lore.
By himself three shall he dress
To cut upon the lord's mess.
Small towel upon his neck shall be seen,
To cleanse his knives that be so keen.

De Elemosinario [1]

The almoner by this hath said grace
And the alms-dish has set in place;
Therein the carver a loaf shall set
To serve God first without let;
These other loaves he pares about,
Lays it amid dish without a doubt;
The small loaf he cuts even in twain
The over-dole [2] in two he lays again.
The almoner a rod shall have in hand,
As office for alms, I understand.
All the broken meat he keeps, I wot,
To deal to poor men at the gate;
And drink that is left served in hall,
Of rich and poor, both great and small.
He is sworn to oversee the service well,

[1] *Of the Almoner.*   [2] Upper part.

And deal it to the poor every deal.
Silver he deals riding by the way,
And his alms dish, as I you say,
To the poorest man that he can find,
Or else, I wot, he is unkind.

De Ferculario [1]

This while the squire to kitchen shall go away,
And bring above meat for assay.
The cook assays the meat undight,
The sewer, he takes and covers aright.
Whosoever takes that meat to bear,
Shall not be so hardy the coverture to rear,
For cold nor hot, I warn you all,
For suspicion of treason, as may befall.
If the silver dish be over hot,
A subtlety I will that thou wot :
Take the bread carven [2] and lay between,
And keep thee well it be not seen ;
I teach it for no courtesy,
But for thine ease [3]—

[1] *Of the Sewer.*   Literally, food-bearer.
[2] Cut bread.   [3] Line unfinished.

When the sewer comes unto the board,
All the meat he assays at a bare word,
The pottage first with bread y-carven,[1]
Covers them again lest they be starven ; [2]
With fish or flesh if they be served,
A morsel thereof for him shall be craved,
And touches the mess over all about ;
The sewer it eats without a doubt.
With baken meat, if he served be so,
The lids up-reared ere he further go :
The pasty or pie he assays within,
Dips bread in gravy, no more no myn.[3]
If the baked meat be cold as may befall,
A gobbet of the same he assays withal.
But thou that bearest meat in hand,
If the sewer stand, look thou stand,
If he kneel, kneel thou so long for aught,
Till meat be assayed that thou hast brought.
As oft at high board, if of bread be need,
The butler two loaves takes indeed,
That one sets down, that other again
He bears to cupboard in towel plain.[4]

[1] Cut.   [2] Cold. See note.   [3] Less.   [4] Simply.

As oft as the carver fetches drink,
The butler assays it, how good him think.
In the lord's cup what is left undrunk,
Into the alms-dish it shall be sunk.
The carver anon without thought,
Uncovers the cup that he has brought,
Into the coverture wine he pours out,
Or into a spare piece without doubt,
Assays and gives the lord to drink,
Or sets it down, as good him think.
The carver shall carve the lord's meat,
Of what sort of piece that he will eat ; [1]
And on his trencher he it lays,
In this manner, without displays.
In alms-dish he lays each deal,
That he is served with at the meal,
Unless he send to any stranger,
A piece that is him lief and dear ; [1]
And send him his pottage also,
That shall not to the alms go.
Of carver more if must I tell,
Another fit then must I spell ;

[1] See note.

Therefore I let it here over pass,
To make our talking some deal less.
When the lord has eaten, the sewer shall bring
The surnape on his shoulder to him,
A narrow towel, a broad beside,
And off his hands he lets it slide.
The usher leads that one end right,
The almoner the other away shall dight.
When the usher comes to the end of the board,
The narrow towel he stretches well toward,
Before the lord and lady so dear ;
Double he folds the towel there.
When they have washen and said is grace,
Away he takes the towel apace,
Lowers the board unto the floor,
Takes away the trestles that be so store.[1]

De Candelario [2]

Now will I speak a little while,
Of the chandler, without guile,
That torches and tapers and prickets can make,
Perchers,[3] small candles, I undertake ;

[1] Great.　　[2] *Of the Chandler.*　　[3] Paris, *i.e.*, large candles.

Of wax these candles all that bren,
And mortar of wax, as I well ken.
The snuff of them he does away
With close scissors, as I you say.
The scissors be short and closed round,
With plate of iron on the end bound.
In chamber no light there shall be brent,
But of wax thereto, if ye take tent.
In hall at supper shall candles bren
Of Paris, therein that all men ken,
Each mess a candle from All Hallows' Day,
To Candlemas, as I you say.
Of candles delivery squires shall have
So long if it is that man will crave.
Of bread and ale also the butler,
Shall make delivery throughout the year,
To squires, and also wine to knight,
Or else he does not his office right.
Here endeth the third speech.
Of all our sins Christ be our leech,
And bring us to his dwelling-place !
" Amen," say ye, for his great grace.

                              Amen, par charite.

SYMON'S LESSON OF WISDOM FOR ALL MANNER CHILDREN

ALL manner children, ye listen and hear
    A lesson of wisdom that is written clear.
My child, I advise thee be wise, take heed of this rhyme,
Which old men in proverb said in old time :
" A child were better to be unborn
Than to be untaught and so to be lorn."
The child that has his will alway,
Shall thrive late, I thee well say.
And therefore, every good man's child,
That is too wanton and too wild,
Learn well this lesson certainly,
That thou the better man may be.
Child, I warn thee in all wise,
That thou tell truth and make no lies.
Child, be not froward, be not proud,
But hold up thy head and speak aloud ;
And when any man speaketh to thee
Doff thy hood and bow thy knee.
And wash thy hands and thy face,
And be courteous in every place.

And when thou comest where is good cheer
In hall or bower, bid " God be here ! "
Look thou cast to no man's dog,
With staff nor stone at horse nor hog.
Look that thou not scorn nor jape
Neither with man, maiden nor ape.
Let no man of thee make plaint.
Swear not by God, neither by saint.
Look thou be courteous standing at meat,
And that men giveth thee, take and eat.
And look thou neither cry nor crave,
Saying, " That and that would I have ! "
But stand thou still before the board,
And look thou speak no loud word.
And child, worship thy father and thy mother ;
Look that thou grieve neither one nor other,
But ever, among them thou shalt kneel down,
And ask their blessing and benison.
And child, keep thy clothes fair and clean ;
Let no foul filth on them be seen.
Child, climb not over house nor wall,[1]
For no fruit, birds nor ball.

[1] See note.

Child, over men's houses no stones fling,
Nor at glass windows no stones sling.
Nor make no crying, jokes, nor plays
In holy church on holy days.
And child, I warn thee of another thing,
Keep thee from many words and wrangling.
And child, when thou goest to play,
Look thou come home by light of day.
And child, I warn thee of another matter,
Look thou keep thee from fire and water.
Be ware and wise how that thou look
Over any brink, well, or brook.
And when thou standest at any schate [1]
Be ware and wise that thou catch no stake ;
For many child without dread,
Through evil heed is deceived or dead.
Child, keep thy book, cap, and gloves,
And all thing that thee behoves.

.   .   .   .   .   .

Child, be thou neither liar nor thief,
Be thou no meecher [2] for mischief.
Child, make thou no mows nor knacks,[3]

[1] Fence. See note.   [2] Whiner.   [3] Tricks.

Before no men nor behind their backs.
But be of fair semblance and countenance,
For by fair manners men may thee advance.
Child, when thou goest in any street,
If thou any good man or woman meet,
Avale [1] thy hood to him or to her,
And bid " God speed, dame, or sir ! "
And be they small or great thou hast met,
This lesson that thou not forget ;
For it is seemly to every man's child,
And mannerly, to clerks to be meek and mild.
And child, rise betimes and go to school,
And fare not as wanton [2] fool ;
And learn as fast as thou may and can,
For our bishop is an old man,
And therefore thou must learn fast,
If thou wilt be bishop when he is passed.[3]
Child, I bid thee on my blessing,
That thou forget not this for nothing ;
But look, thou hold it well in thy mind,
For the best thou shalt it find.
For, as the wise man saith and proveth,

[1] Doff.   [2] Ill-bred.   [3] See note.

A wise child, lore he behoveth;
And as men say that learned be,
Who spareth the rod, the child hateth he;
And as the wise man saith in his book,
Of proverbs and wisdoms, who will look:
" As a sharp spur maketh a horse to move,
Under a man that should war prove,
Right so a yard may make a child,
To learn well his lesson and to be mild."
Lo! children, here may ye all hear and see,
How all children chastised should be.
And therefore, childer, look ye do well,
And no hard beating shall you befall.
Thus may ye all be right good men,
God grant you grace so to preserve you!   Amen.
                              [Quoth] SYMON.

HUGH RHODES'S BOOK OF NURTURE AND SCHOOL OF GOOD MANNERS

ALL ye that would learn and then would be calléd wise,
Obedience learn in youth, in age it will avoid vice.

"Who spareth the rod, the child hateth."

I am blind in poet's art, thereof I have no skill ;
All eloquence I put apart, and follow mine own will.

Corrupt in speech my briefs and longs [1] to know,
Born and bred in Devonshire, my terms will well show.

Take the best and leave the worst, of truth I mean no ill;
If the matter be not curious, the intent is good, mark
  it well.

Pardon I ask if I offend thus boldly for to write,
To master or servant (young and old) I do myself
  submit.

I would reform both youth and age, if anything be amiss;
To you will I shew my mind, reform ye where need is.

All that have young people, good manners set them
  to learn ;
To their elders with gentle conditions let do nor say
  no harm.

If they do ill, wise men may report their parents soon ;
How should they teach other good, belike themselves
  can [2] none.

---

[1] Metrical quantities. See note.   [2] Know.

A good father maketh good children, if wisdom be
    them within,
Such as of custom use it in youth, in age they will begin.

He that lacketh good manners is little set by ;
Without virtue or good conditions, a man is not worth
    a fly.

Reverence father and mother (of duty), kind [1] doth
    thee bind ;
Such children increaseth, and likely to recover virtue
    by kind. [1]

Against father and mother multiply no words, be
    you [2] sure ;
It will be to thee laud and to thy friends joyful to hear.

A plant without moisture may not bring forth his
    flower ;
If youth be void of virtue, in age he shall lack honour.

First dread God, next flee sin, all earthly things are
    mortál ;
Stand not too fast in thy conceit, for pride will have a
    fall.

[1] Nature.   [2] See note.

Use early rising in the morning, for it hath properties
    three ;
Holy, healthy, wealthy—in my youth thus my father
    taught me.

At six of the clock at farthest, accustom thee to rise ;
Look thou forget not to bless thee once or twice.

In the morning use some devotion, and let for no need ;
Then all the day afterward the better shalt thou speed.

.   .   .   .   .   .

Sponge and brush thy clothes clean that thou shalt on
    wear ;
Cast up your bed, and take heed ye lose none of your
    gear.

Make clean thy shoes, comb thy head, mannerly thee
    brace ;
See thou forget not to wash both thy hands and face.

Put on thy clothing for thy degree,[1] honestly do it
    make.
Bid your fellow good morrow, ere ye your way forth
    take.

[1] According to thy station.

To your friends and to father and mother look ye take
  heed ;
For any haste do them reverence, the better shalt
  thou speed.

Dread the cursing of father and mother, for it is a
  heavy thing ;
Do thy duty to them, the contrary will be to thy
  dispraising.

When thy father and mother come in sight, do them
  reverénce,
And ask them blessing if they have been long out of
  presénce.

Cleanly appoint you your array, beware then of disdain;
Then be gentle of speech and mannerly you retain.

And as ye pass the town or street, sadly [1] go forth your
  way,
[Nor] gaze nor scoff, nor scold, with man nor child
  make no fray.

Fair speech doth great pleasure ; it seemeth of gentle
  blood ;
Gentle is to use fair speech ; it requireth nothing
  but good.

[1] Soberly.

And when thou comest into the church thy prayers
    for to say,
Kneel, sit, stand or walk, devoutly look thou pray.

Cast not your eye to and fro, all things for to see ;
Then shalt thou be judged plainly a wanton for to be.

When thou art in the church, [see thou] do churchly
    works ;
Communication use thou not to women, priests nor
    clerks.

When your devotion is done and time is toward dinner ;
Draw home to your master's presence, there do your
    [en]deavour.

An ye be desired to serve, or sit, or eat meat at the table,
Incline to good manners, and to nurture yourself enable.

If your sovereign call you with him to dine or sup,
Give him reverence to begin, both of meat and cup.

And beware for anything, press [1] not thyself too
    high ;
To sit in the place appointed thee—that is courtesy.

[1] Praise (1550), prease (1568, 1577).

And when thou art set, and table served thee before,
Pare not your nails, 'file [1] not your cloth—learn ye
that lore.

An thy master speak to thee, take thy cap in hand,
If thou sit at meat, when he talketh [to thee] see thou
stand.

Lean not to the one side when thou speakest, for
nothing,
Hold still both hand and foot, and beware of trifling.

Stand sadly [2] in telling thy tale whenas thou talkest ;
Trifle with nothing, and stand upright when thou
speakest.

Thwart [3] not thou with thy fellow, nor speak with high
voice ;
Point not thy tale with thy fingers, use not such
toys. [4]

Have audience when thou speakest, speak with
authority,
Else if thou speak wisdom, little will it avail thee.

[1] Defile.   [2] Soberly.
[3] Don't cross thy fellow.   [4] Tricks.

Pronounce thy speech with a pause, mark well thy word;
It is good hearing a child; beware with whom ye bourd.[1]

Talk not to thy sovereign, no time when he doth
    drink;
When he speaketh, give him audience—that is good, I
    think.

Before that you sit, see that your knife be bright,
Your hands clean, your nails pared is a good sight.

When thou shalt speak, roll not too fast thine eye;
Gaze not to and fro, as one that were void of courtesy.

For a man's countenance often times declareth his
    thought;
His look with his speech will judge him, good or naught.

And see your knife be sharp to cut your meat withal;
So the more cleanlier cut your meat you shall.

Ere thou put much bread in thy pottage, look thou it
    assay;
Fill not thy spoon too full, lest thou lose somewhat
    by the way.

[1] Jest.

If men eat of your dish, crumb therein no bread,
Lest your hands be sweaty, thereof take ye good heed.

They may be corrupt[1] that causeth it, it is no fair
uságe.
Of bread slice out fair morsels to put in your pottáge.

Fill it not too full of bread, for it may be to thee
reprovable ;
Lest thou leave part, then to measure thou art
variable.[2]

And sup not loud of thy pottage, no time in all thy
life.
Dip not thy meat in the salt-cellar, but take it with
a knife.

When thou hast eaten thy pottage, do as I shall thee
wish ;
Wipe clean thy spoon and leave it not in thy dish.

Lay it down before thy trencher, thereof be not afraid ;
And take heed who taketh it up, lest it be conveyed.[3]

---

[1] The sweat may be due to disease.
[2] Thou dost sin against moderation.   [3] Stolen.

Cut not the best morsel for thyself, leave part behind.
Be not greedy of meat and drink, be liberal and kind.

Burnish no bones with your teeth, for it is unseemly.
Rend not thy meat asunder, for to courtesy it is
    contrary.

An a stranger sit near thee, ever among now and then,
Reward him with some dainties, like a gentleman.

If thy fellow sit from his meat, and cannot come thereto,
Then cut him such as thou hast, that is gently [to] do.

Belch near no man's face with a corrupt fumosity ; [1]
Turn from such occasion, it is a stinking ventosity.[2]

Eat small morsels of meat, not too great in quantity,
If ye like such meats, yet follow not ever thy phantasy.[3]

Corrupt not thy lips with eating, as a pig in draff ;
Eat softly and drink mannerly ; beware ye do not quaff.

Scratch not thy head with [4] thy fingers, when thou
    art at meat,
Nor spit you over the table-board, see thou do not
    forget.

[1] Smoke ; here, breath.   [2] Gas.
[3] See note.   [4] Ed. 1577, or.

Pick not thy teeth with thy knife nor finger-end,
But with a stick [1] or some clean thing, then do ye not
  offend.

If your teeth be putrified, methinks it is no right
To touch meat that other should eat, it is no cleanly
  sight.

Pick not thy hands nor play with thy knife ;
Keep still foot and hand ; at meat begin ye no
  strife.

Wipe thy mouth when thou shalt drink ale or wine
On thy napkin only ; and see all things be clean.

Blow not your nose in the napkin where ye wipe your
  hand ;
Cleanse it in your handkerchief, then pass ye not your
  band. [2]

With your napkin you may oft wipe your mouth clean ;
Something thereon will cleave that cannot be seen.

Fill not thy trencher with morsels great and large ;
With much meat fill not thy mouth like a barge.

[1] See note.
[2] The sense is apparently: soil . your wristband.

Temper thyself with drink, so keep thee from blame;
It [1] hurteth thy honesty and hindereth thy good name.

A pint at a draught to pour in fast, as one in haste,
Four at a mess is three too many,[2] in such I think waste.

Use thy self from excess, both in meat and drink;
And ever keep temperance, whether [3] you wake or wink.

Fill not thy mouth too full, lest thou must needs speak,
Nor blow out thy crumbs when thou doëst eat.

Foul not the place with spitting whereas thou doëst sit,
Lest it abhor some to see it when thou hast forgot.

If thou must spit, or blow thy nose, keep it out of sight,
Let it not lie on ground, but tread it out right.

With bones and void [4] morsels fill not thy trencher too
full;
Avoid [4] them into a voider,[4] and no man will it null.[5]

Roll not thy meat in thy mouth, that every man may it
see;
But eat thy meat somewhat close, for it is honesty.

---

[1] Drink. Later editions have *drunkenness*.
[2] Four pints of ale.   [3] Ed. 1577.
[4] Void = cast-off; avoid = empty; voider = receptacle to
take cast-off morsels.   [5] Annul, *i.e.*, object to it.

If thy sovereign proffer thee to drink once, twice or
     thrice,
Take it gently at his hand, for in court it is the guise.

When thou has drunk, set it down or take it to his
     servánt ;
Let not thy master set it down, then it is well, I
     warránt.

Blow not in thy pottage or drink, that is not com-
     mendáble,
For an thou be not whole of body, thy breath is
     corruptíble.[1]

Cast not thy bones under the table, nor none do thou
     knack.[2]
Stretch thee not at the table, nor lean forth thy
     back.

Afore dinner or after, with thy knife score[3] not the
     board ;
Such toys are not commendable, trust me at a word.

Lean not on the board when your master is thereat ;
For then will your sovereign think in you checkmate.[4]

----

[1] Unpleasant.   [2] Gnaw.
[3] Scratch.   [4] See note.

Be not ashamed to eat the meat which is set before
    thee;
Mannerly for to take it, that agreeth well with courtesy.

Cast not thine eyes to and fro, as one that were full of
    toys;
Much wagging with the head seemeth thou art not
    wise.

Scratch not thy head, put thou not thy finger in thy
    mouth;
Blow not thy nose, nor look thereon; to some it is loth.

Be not loud where you be, nor at the table where ye sit;
Some men will deem thee drunken or mad, or to lack
    wit.

When meat is taken away, and the voiders set in
    presénce,
Put your trencher in the voider, and also the residénce.[1]

Take with your napkin and knife forth crumbs before
    thee;
Put your napkin in the voider, for it is courtesy.

Your square of trencher-bread, together with the scraps
upon it.

Be gentle alway and good to please, be it night or day,
With tongue and hand, be not 'ragious;[1] let reason
    rule alway.

When the meat is taken up and the tablecloth made
    clean,
Then take heed of grace, and to wash yourself demean.

And while grace is saying, see ye make no noise;
Thank God of your fare, to your sovereign give praise.

When ye perceive to rise, say to your fellows all,
"Much good do it you," gently, then gentle, men
    will you call.

Then go to your sovereign, and give obeisance mannerly,
And withdraw you aside, as best for your honesty.

An ye see men in great counsel, press not too near;
They will say you are untaught; that is sure and
    clear.

Speak not much in thy fellow's ear, give no ill language;
Men are suspicious, and will think it no good usage.

[1] Outrageous.

Laugh not too much at the table, nor make at it no
    game.

Avoid slanderous and bawdy tales; use them not for
    shame.

Ere thou be old, beware, so thou may'st get a sudden
    fall;

An you be honest in youth, in age ye may be liberal.

FRANCIS SEAGER'S SCHOOL OF VIRTUE

THE AUTHOR'S NAME INVERTED

S   ay well some will   by this my labour,

E   very man yet   will not say the same.

A   mong the good   I doubt not favour;

G   od them forgive   [that] for it me blame.

E   ach man I wish   [whom] it shall offend,

R   ead and then judge,   where fault is, amend.

Face aut Tace

FIRST in the morning,   when thou dost awake,

To God for His grace,   thy petition then make.

This prayer following   use daily to say;

Thy heart lifting up,   thus begin to pray.

The Morning Prayer

" O God from whom — all good gifts proceed,
To thee we repair — in time of our need,
That with thy grace — thou wouldst us endue,
Virtue to follow — and vice to eschew.
Hear this our request, — and grant our desire,
O Lord, most humbly — we do thee require.
This day us defend — that we walking aright
May do the thing — acceptable in thy sight;
That as we in years — and body do grow,
So in good virtues — we may likewise flow
To thy honour — and joy of our parents,
Learning to live well — and keep thy command-
ments,

In flying from all — vice, sin and crime,
Applying our books, — not losing our time,
May fructify and go forward — here in good doing,
In this vale of misery — unto our lives' ending;
That after this life — here transitory,
We may attain — to greater glory."

The Lord's prayer then — see thou recite,
So using to do, — at morning and night.

How to Order Thyself when Thou Risest and in Apparelling thy Body

Fly ever sloth	and overmuch sleep ;
In health the body	thereby thou shalt keep.
Much sleep engendereth	diseases and pain,
It dulls the wit	and hurteth the brain.
Early in the morning,	thy bed then forsake,
Thy raiment put on,	thyself ready make.
To cast up thy bed	it shall be thy part,
Else may they say	that beastly thou art ;
So to depart	and let the same lie,
It is not seeming	nor yet mannerly.
Down from thy chamber	when thou shalt go,
Thy parents salute thou,	and the family also ;
Thy hands see thou wash,	and thy head comb,
And of thy raiment	see torn be no seam ;
Thy cap fair brushed,	thy head cover then,
Taking it off,	in speaking to any man.
Cato doth council thee	thine elders to reverence,
Declaring thereby	thy duty and obedience.
Thy shirt collar fast	to thy neck knit ;
Comely thy raiment	look on thy body sit ;

Thy girdle about   thy waist then fasten,
Thy hose fair rubbed,   thy shoes see be clean.
A napkin see that   thou have in readiness,
Thy nose to cleanse   from all filthiness.
Thy nails, if need be,   see that thou pare ;
Thine ears keep clean,   thy teeth wash thou fair
If aught about thee   chance to be torn,
Thy friends thereof show how it is worn,
And they will new   for thee provide,
Or the old mend,   in time being spied.
This done, thy satchell   and thy books take,
And to the school   haste see thou make.
But ere thou go,   with thyself forethink.
That thou take with thee pen, paper and ink ;
For these are things   for thy study necessáry,
Forget not then   with thee them to carry.
The soldier preparing   himself to the field,
Leaves not at home   his sword and his shield ;
No more should a scholar forget then truly
What he at school   should need to occupy.[1]
These things thus had,   take straight thy way,
Unto the school   without any stay.

[1] Use.

they remain, and for the more true and zealous calling unto Thee for these things, give me grace in faith to say that prayer which Thy Son Jesus Christ hath taught me, saying "O our Father which art in Heaven," &c.

FINIS

NOTES

THE BABEES' BOOK

MS. Harleian 5086, fols. 86–90, about 1475, ends, "Learn or be lewd." First printed by Dr. Furnivall. Nothing is known of the author. Written in *rhyme royal*, five-stress lines in seven-line stanzas, arranged ababbcc. The treatise is noteworthy chiefly in that it seems to be addressed to young princes, and the MS. dates from the time when Edward V. and Richard of York were boys. As it is more tedious than quaint in the original, it has been rendered into prose.

p. 1. *Facet.* For author and title, see *Introduction*, p. xii. It was printed very frequently in the fifteenth and sixteenth centuries, both separately and in connection with seven similar works, two of them also attributed to John Garland, under the title: *Auctores Octo Opusculorum cum commentariis.* &c.; *Videlicet Cathonis, Theodoli, Faceti, Cartule, alias de Contemptu Mundi, Thobiadis, Parabolarum Alani, Fabularum Esopi, Floreti.* The English author seems to have borrowed little besides the name and the introduction,

> "Cum nihil utilius humane credo saluti
> Quam rerum nouisse modos et moribus uti."

p. 2. *Babies.* Children much older than those we associate with the word. Apparently it was used like the Spanish *menino* (French *menin*, introduced from Spain, 1680) to mean, "young man of good family."

p. 2. *Ease in learning*, *i.e.*, because it was in verse.

p. 2. *Lady Facetia.* Apparently the author's feminine of Facetus (perhaps through confusion with *facetiæ*, jokes), because courtesy was usually personified as a woman. In the *Tesoretto*, the chief virtue is Larghezza (liberality), upon whom Courtesy attends, together with Good-Faith and Valour, over against the masculine qualities, Prudence, Temperance, Fortitude, Justice.

p. 3. *Bele.* Fr. *belle*, beautiful. Not common in English (see N. E. D.) until the seventeenth century.

p. 6. *Trencher.* Originally, a slice of wholemeal bread, four days old, upon which food was served. Later, it was made of wood.

p. 8. *Where they ought to be.* In a knife-rack or case? See Wright, *Domestic Manners and Customs*, p. 464.

THE A B C OF ARISTOTLE

MS. Lambeth 853, fol. 30, about 1430, written without breaks; Harl. 5086, fol. 70b, and Harl. 1304, fol. 103, about 1450 (printed in *Queene Eliz. Achad.*). It is needless to say that nothing of the sort is found in Aristotle; the author is unknown. The introduction is in connected alliterative verse (lacking in Harl. 5086, and expanded into a generalised religious discourse in Harl. 1304).

p. 10. *Elenge.* See N. E. D. on this rare word. Its two originally distinct meanings (1) long, hence, tedious, and (2) lonely, remote, combine to form a third meaning, melancholy.

URBANITATIS

MS. Cotton Caligula, A ii, fol. 88, 1446–60. Author unknown. Apparently first printed by Dr. Furnivall. The Duke of Norfolk, grandfather of Anne Boleyn and Katherine Howard, was among the young henchmen at the court of Edward IV., brought up on "the booke of urbanitie."

p. 13. *Good manners*, &c. William of Wykeham was more curt in his motto for Winchester College: "Manners makyth man."

p. 14. *Close your hand*, &c., *i.e.*, one hand over the over, to keep a secret.

p. 14. *Had I wist.* Proverbial. See notes on *The Good Wife*, p. 186, below.

p. 15. *Let your right shoulder*, &c., *i.e.*, keep a step behind him to the left.

THE LITTLE CHILDREN'S LITTLE BOOK

MSS. Harl. 541, fol. 210, and Egerton 1995, about 1480. Sub-title *Edyllys be. Edyllys* may be the O. E. *æthele*, German *edel*, meaning *noble*; but the sentence is then incomplete. Ends "Quod Whytyng." Whether he was author or scribe I do not know, more probably the latter. I have kept the rhyme in this version, because it is at once shorter and more interesting than the other.

p. 16. *Seven Arts.* The quadrivium: arithmetic, music, geometry, astronomy; and the trivium: grammar, rhetoric, logic.

p. 16. *When Gabriel . . . meet.* It is interesting to note that a medieval writer connected courtesy with the worship of Mary, even although he includes no precepts which touch upon what we call chivalry to-day.

p. 16. *Villainy.* The French equivalent of churlishness; what Russell calls " simple conditions."

p. 17. *Beginning . . . think.* This kind of rhyme, not uncommon in the fifteenth century, seems to indicate a pronunciation as in the cockney *nothink.*

p. 17. *Mess.* Here *food*, but sometimes *table* (Latin *mensa*), and again *group of people at a table*, as used still in the expression " officers' mess."

p. 17. *Fault.* Text: that thy salt holds—which the rhyme shows to be corrupt.

p. 18. *Work.* Text: keep—changed for the rhyme.

p. 18. *Fingers,* i.e., not with thy knife? Or has a negative been omitted?

p. 19. *No drop be seen.* So Chaucer's *Prioress.* See *Introduction*, p. xvi.

p. 19. *Behind no man's back.* There was perhaps originally an idea of greed, or, it may be, of possible tampering with the drink, behind the prohibition.

p. 20. *Jill.* From Gillian, once a common name for women.

p. 20. *The same.* Text: in same (German *zusammen*) together.

p. 21. *Cumbered with no fiends.* This fear was very real in the Middle Ages, and was fostered by such stories as *Robert the Devil, Sir Gowther,* and ballads of supernatural beings.

THE YOUNG CHILDREN'S BOOK

MS. Ashmole 61 (Bodleian Library), fol. 20, about 1500.

p. 21. *Seven Sciences*, *i.e.*, knowledges, hence Arts. The introduction is nearly identical, but very few of the maxims agree.

p. 22. *What you get with your hands.* One of the many allusions which suggest adaptation to the middle class. Others are to buying and selling, to getting your money honestly, &c. The stress upon morals rather than manners is perhaps due to the same cause.

p. 25. *At the school.* The inference seems to be that they would learn manners there.

p. 25. *Quoth Kate.* The same name occurs at the end of the three next poems as they appear in MS. Ashmole 61. It is probably a corruption, unless we have here one of the rare instances of a woman copyist. *Cato* suggests itself as the most likely original; and in this way. He was undoubtedly identified with the *Wise Man*, as appears from the *Luytel Caton* of the Vernon MS. (see p. 189, below). Accordingly, *Quod Cato* might have stood at the end of this poem, and have become confused with Kate from Katharine or Catherine.

STANS PUER AD MENSAM

This must have been a popular form of the maxims, as many MSS. still exist. The translation is made from MS. Lambeth 853, fol. 150, about 1430, with occasional references to Harl. 2251, fol. 153 (148), about 1460 (?). A much longer and more tedious (250 lines, instead of 99) version was printed by Dr. Furnivall in *Queene Eliz. Achad.*, from MS. Ashmole 61. This last quotes *Grossum Caput, i.e.*, Grossetete, and refers several times to "Dr. Palere," of whom nothing seems to be known. The Ashmole version, however, contains several interesting points not mentioned in the other two :—

> "Thy elbow and arms have in thy thought,
>   Too far on the table do them not lay."

> "And if thou see any man reading a letter,
>   Come not too nigh him for dread of blame."

"And if thou go with any man in field or in town,
  By wall or by hedge, by palace or by pale,
To go without (outside) him, look thou be bown (ready),
  And take him betwixt thee and that same wall ;
And if thou meet him, look thou be sure
  That thou go without him, and leave him next the
    wall."

> "Stare not on a strange man too much, be thou ware."

> "Nor never mock an old man, though he be old."

Various other MSS. are (1) Jesus College, Cambridge (Q.T. 8, printed by Wright & Halliwell, in *Reliquiæ Antiquæ*, I., 156–58), (2) Cotton Caligula A ii, Harl. 4011, Lansdowne 699, Additional 5467, &c. It was printed once by Caxton, and several times by Wynkyn de Worde.

The only reason for considering John Lydgate as the author lies in the attribution to him in the last stanza (see next page).

p. 27. *Indict.* Text: edwite, modern, twit.
p. 30. *Ah, little ballad,* &c.   The Harl. text reads:

"Go, little bill, barren of eloquence,
    Pray young children that thee shall see or read,
Though thou be compendious of sentence,
    Of thy clauses for to take heed,
    Which to all virtue shall their youth lead.
Of the writing, though there be no date,
    If aught be amiss in word, syllable, or deed,
Put all the default upon John Lydgate."

HOW THE GOOD WIFE TAUGHT
HER DAUGHTER

MS. Lambeth 853, p. 102, about 1430, written without
breaks.   Other MSS. are Trinity College, Cambridge,
R. 3, 19, and Ashmole 61, p. 7 (printed in *Queene Elizabethes
Achademy*), a later and inferior text, which contains, however, a fresh and interesting stanza:

"And if it thus thee betide,
    That friends fail thee on every side,
    And God from thee thy child take,
    Thy wreak (vengeance) on God thou must not take,
    For thyself it will undo
    And all thews (virtues) that thee 'longs to.
    Many a one for her own folly,
    Spills (destroys) themselves unthriftily."

MS. Porkington 10, p. 135 back, about 1460-70 con-
tained a variant form *The Good Wife Would a Pilgrimage,*

i.e., before she sets out for the Holy Land, she leaves instructions for her daughter. This version (printed in *Queene Eliz. Achad.*) is interesting for its proverbs:

> "The loth (hated) child behoves lore,
> And lief child much more."

> "Seldom mosseth the stone,
> That oft is turned and wend."

> "A fool's bolt is soon shot
> And doth but little good."

> "When deed is done, it is too late;
> Beware of 'Had I wist.'"

A third version was printed in 1597 under the title, *The Northern Mother's Blessing*. Written nine years before the death of G. Chaucer. Together with it a short poem: *The Way to Thrift*. This contains several different and interesting stanzas.

It begins:

> "God would that every wife that dwelleth in this land,
> Would teach her daughter as ye shall understand,
> As a good wife did of the North countré
> How her daughter should learn a good wife to be:
> For lack of the mother's teaching
> Makes the daughter of evil living,
> My lief dear child."

Another is:

> "In other men's houses make thee no mastery,
> Nor blame thou nothing thou sees with thine eye;
> Daughter, I thee pray, bear thee so well
> That all men may say thou art true as steel;

For wise men and old
Say good name is worth gold,
      My lief dear child.

Sit not at even too long at gaze with the cup,
For to wassail and drink all up ;
So to bed betimes, at morn rise belive,
And so may thou better learn to thrive.
      He that will a good house keep,
      Must oft times break a sleep,
            My lief dear child.

If it betide, daughter, thy friend from thee fall,
And God send thee children that for bread will call,
And thou have mickle need, help little or none,
Thou must then care and spare, hard as the stone—
      For evil that may betide,
      A man before should dread,
            My lief dear child."

The order of the stanzas is different from that here
printed.

The rhyme-scheme is normally aabbccd ; but the first,
second, seventeenth, and last stanzas are irregular—abcddc,
ababcdcdeef, aabbccdde, and aaaa, thus varying in both
number and arrangement of lines. The first four verses
contain roughly the same number of accents, the fifth and
sixth vary greatly in length, while the seventh is a con-
stant refrain to all stanzas except the first and last.

The poem is distinctly popular in tone ; and I have
seldom attempted to improve its rough metre, holding
that the effect is racier as it is.

p. 31. *Kirk.* Text has *church*, but the rhyme is *work.*

p. 32. *Thrive . . . life.* The corresponding couplets are usually proverbial in character.

p. 33. *Whatsoever he be.* Apparently on the basis that "e'er a man is better than ne'er a man."

p. 33. *Atterling.* Literally, one who deals in poisons (O. E. *ator*); hence, a witch; hence, a shrew.

p. 34. *Maze.* Without the help of the N. E. D., the word is puzzling; but the context seems to demand *maze*, connected with *amaze*, rather than *maze=labyrinth.*

p. 35. *Shooting at the cock.* The popular old English pastime of throwing missiles to bring down a cock tied by the leg.

p. 37. *Deed . . . speed.* The meaning is that a deed finished quickly helps on another by giving place to it.

p. 38. *Term-day.* Servants were hired by the year at special times which varied according to the district, being usually coincident with the big fairs of that part. Michaelmas was a usual time.

p. 40. *As a wren hath veins.* The wren is so small that but little blood can be let from her veins. Put more strongly: "You cannot squeeze blood out of a stone."

HOW THE WISE MAN TAUGHT HIS SON

Found in various MSS. The version in *The Babees' Book* is printed from Lambeth 853, fol. 186. Another is given in *Queene Eliz. Achad.* from Ashmole 61, fol. 6. Ritson, in his *Ancient Popular Poetry*, printed Harl. 4596, and Hazlitt, in his *Early Popular Poetry*, MS. Camb. Ff. ii. *Luytel Caton*

(Part II., Minor Poems of the Vernon MS., published by Dr. Furnivall, 1902) says : —

> "Now whoso will, he may hear
>   In English language,
>   How the Wise Man taught his Son,
>   That was of tender age" (ll. 5–8).

It is doubtful whether this poem was written in imitation of the preceding, or that of this, but the *Wise Man*, through its connection with Cato, has the longer pedigree. A poem in the *Exeter Book* begins: "Thus a wise father (*frodfæder*) instructed his dear son, a parent wise in mind, old in virtues, sagacious in words," &c. Although I have not been able to compare the different versions in detail, I incline to believe that there are recognisable links between them all. *The Good Wife* is, however, much the more vivid and amusing of the two.

The metre is ababbcbc, but the poem loses little by being turned into prose.

p. 47. *All that there is.* This passage suggests one in the *Blickling Homilies* (No. VIII. *Soul's Need*, ed. Morris), which goes back to St. Augustine.

JOHN RUSSELL'S BOOK OF NURTURE

First printed by Dr. Furnivall from MS. Harl. 4011, fols. 171–89, dated about 1460. Other copies are in Sloane 1315, fols. 49–67 and 2027, fols. 1–15b, supposed to be slightly earlier in date; also, Royal 17 D xv., article 5.

Nothing is known of the author beyond what he himself says, that he was usher and marshal to Duke Humphrey of Gloucester (regent during the minority of Henry VI.). He was seemingly an old man and a widower before the death of Duke Humphrey, who was murdered in 1447. This seems to be suggested by the fact that he asks the reader's prayers for Duke Humphrey (as the King is prayed for to-day) and then for the souls of his wife and his parents. If then he was forced to retire from court by old age (as he says in another place, see p. 77, above) some time before 1447, he might have been born even before 1360, and studied his courtesy under Edward III., or at the very latest under Richard II.

The device of wandering in the country and there meeting with some one who furnishes the subject of the poem was extensively used by Chaucer and his school, derived by them in turn from French poets of the thirteenth century.

The long lines and pompous metre which he uses I have employed occasionally, where the subject permitted that form, to show the effect. The whole production done that way would become insufferably tedious.

p. 49. "Is thy governance good?" Practically, "Do you behave well?"

p. 50. *Smooth and square the trenchers with.* At this time, still made of stale wholemeal bread; later, of wood.

p. 51. *Linen clouts.* To stop up holes?

p. 52. *Couleur de rose.* A red wine, classified under malmsey (and therefore Greek?), mentioned in the *Interlude of the Four Elements.*

p. 52. *New ale is wasteful,* i.e., people can drink so much of it because it is not intoxicating.

p. 52. *Stale drink.* Perhaps an allusion to the lead

poisoning which is known to result from drinking ale that has stood in a pewter pot for some time.

p. 52. *Cowche.* Any sort of cover. Used perhaps as nowadays to lessen the noise and save the board.

p. 53. *Lay a second cloth.* I understand this to mean that one linen cloth was not wide enough to cover the table and to hang down sufficiently; hence, that two were used, overlapping in the middle, and hanging down on each side. By following the directions, literally, it is possible to see what is meant. The *outer* edge, I take to be that nearest the centre of the room, the *inner*, next to the wall.

p. 53. *State.* A fold or some other ornamental arrangement of the table-cloth. The usher or sewer seems to have twisted or curled it with his rod.

p. 53. *Put a towel round your neck.* The achievement described in the following lines is quite possible, if the loaves are small, and makes quite a "mannerly" appearance.

p. 54. *Rennes cloth.* Made at Rennes in Brittany, and frequently mentioned in the romances.

p. 54. *Fold it lengthwise,* &c. This performance was possibly to give an appearance of cleanliness. The best way to understand the process is to take a towel and try; it is not so complicated as it sounds.

p. 55. *Surnape.* This again becomes simple by experiment. The pleat or doubling about a foot from the end of the table, is probably to avoid letting the long cloth fall to the floor. When the triple thickness of cloth has been pushed and pulled across the table by the butler and marshal, the pleat is smoothed out and the cloth hangs from eighteen to thirty inches over each end.

p. 55. *Sewer.* Fr. *esculier*, Lat. *scutellarius*, whence also is derived *scullery*. The sewer's office was practically to bring and arrange the dishes.

p. 57. *Winking and watering*. More or less difficult in the days of primitive chimneys, or no chimneys at all.

p. 60. *Upper crust*. In the old ovens, which were heated by faggots withdrawn before the bread was put in, this was even more distinctly the best part.

p. 60. *Carving of flesh*, &c. This more properly belongs in a book given over to recipes and the like, as the description of the dishes is more interesting than the special knack of serving each one.

p. 62. *Need not fear*, &c. Almost the only suggestion of any indignity in the service.

p. 63. *He   and look you*. The change of person is Russell's.

p. 63. *As brown as a water-leech.* Is the allusion possibly to shoes of dark-brown colour? Leeches are usually described as black.

p. 65. *Bankers.* Translated *bench-covers;* but the context suggests rather *bolsters.* The bench-covers were doubtless cushions; hence the transition from the one meaning to the other is easy.

p. 67. *By the license of his estate.* This seems to point to a Sumptuary Law. In 1483, it was decreed that none under the rank of a lord might wear cloth of gold, none under a knight, velvet, &c.

p. 67. *Wound.* A sort of turban?

p. 67. *Paris-candle* or *percher.* A big candle of the sort commonly used on altars.

p. 68. *Medicinable Bath.* A sort of Turkish bath with herbs added. Some of those mentioned were known for their curative properties, even in Saxon times, as holly-hock, mallow, centaury, fennel, heyriff, daisy, brooklime, ribwort, flax, willow. Mallow was supposed to be good for wounds. Wall pellitory contains nitrate of potash. Fennel is still used as a home remedy. Heyhove is bitter and aromatic, abounding in a principle similar to camphor. Heyriff used to be applied externally for scurvy, and is said to be still used in France (taken internally) for epilepsy. Scabious was once thought valuable for various diseases, primarily the itch, but also coughs, pleurisy, &c. Dane-wort was traditionally thought to have sprung up whenever there had been an encounter between the English and the Danes; it is a dwarf elder valued for its purgative pro-perties. Centaury was so named from the legend that by it Chiron the Centaur was cured. It is gentianaceous and valuable as a bitter. Herb-bennet, *herba benedicta*, the blessed herb, was supposed to be particularly efficacious in keeping away the devil. It was perhaps hemlock, or wild valerian. St. John's wort seems to have been a neutral element, although it may have been added for some special reason. Bresewort or bruisewort is the common daisy, once highly valued for its general medicinal properties. Bugloss (text, *bilgres*) was valued as a blood-purifier. Camomile is still used in home medicine.

p. 70. *Mayor of Calais.* Because this was the one French port that continued to be held by the English after the Hundred Years' War until the reign of Queen Mary. This officer was also called "Mayor of the Staple," because of the wool-trade carried on through Calais. See p. 71, above.

p. 71. *Golden royal rod.* A prince who was crowned in his father's life-time? In 1343, the Black Prince was in-

vested with a gold circlet and ring, and silver rod, by
Edward III.; so, likewise Henry V., in 1399, received a
coronet, ring and golden rod.

p. 72. *Bishop of Canterbury*, &c. This means only that
neither archbishop had jurisdiction over the see of the
other.

p. 73. *Groom, i.e.*, receive each as if he were one degree
higher than his actual estate.

p. 74. *Queenborough.* A small port near the mouth of
the Thames, on the island of Sheppey.

p. 74. *Abbot of Westminster.* The yearly rental, as
quoted by Dr. Furnivall from *Valor Ecclesiarum* I., pp. 410–
24, was £4470, os. 2d.; of Tintern, £258, 5s. 1od. (*Val.
Ecc.* IV., 370–71).

p. 74. *Prior of Dudley.* The value of this quoted by
Dr. Furnivall was £34, 1s. 4d. over against Canterbury at
£163, 1s. 9d. (*Val. Ecc.* III., pp. 4–5, and I., 27–32).

p. 75. *Whether the cook be lief or loth.* A hint that the
cook was not always duly subordinate.

p. 78. "*Go forth, little book,*" &c. The *Envoi* presents a
problem which at present I cannot solve. The question
is, how much of the "copy" here is the same as the
treatise used by Russell in his youth, and whether another
writer adds an *Envoi* explaining how he has improved
Russell's work, while the latter is referring to a still
earlier work. There is every probability that Russell's
own work ends with the request for prayers, which includes the mention of the author's name, and concludes
with *Amen.* And in support of this view is the fact that
neither of the Sloane MSS., which seem earlier than
the one translated, contains either the *Envoi* or Russell's

name. As I have not studied the relation of the MSS. I hesitate to conjecture; but from the facts at my disposal, I think it probable that the writer of the *Envoi* alludes to Russell as the "fore writer," and casts the blame for whatever faults may be found, upon the treatise on which Russell himself declared his work to be based. It would appear also that the writer of the *Envoi* did not recognise Russell's source. This may possibly have been the *Book of Courtesy*, which (especially in its third book) often corresponds to Russell. Moreover, as it was written by a man who talked familiarly of John of Gaunt (see p. 112, above), who died in 1399, it agrees well enough with the date of the book used by Russell in his youth; but, needless to say, there is no proof that they were the same.

THE BOOK OF COURTESY

MS. Sloane 1986, about 1460. The text is either very corrupt, or the style is as rough as possible, lacking even the essentials of grammar. It contains many Scotch words, and has certainly suffered in its rhymes, and probably in its sense through English copyists. The author apparently remembered the institution of a custom at the court of John of Gaunt; hence it seems likely that he wrote before 1420.

p. 81. *Bakes*. Perhaps rolls into a ball or moulds, as this is a stage of baking.

p. 81. *Wallowing*, i.e., rolling the morsel about.

p. 83. *Chare*. From the O. E. verb *to turn*; hence, a

turn either at play as here (trick) or at work, as in the compound *charwoman*.

p. 85. *Cross-Christ thee speed.* The same oath occurs in *Sir Gawayne and the Green Knight*, l. 762; but I do not remember it elsewhere. The order of the first two words is commonly *Christ-cross*, as in "Christ-cross-row" (alphabet). The inversion is possibly a sign of translation from the French.

p. 86. *On both knees.* So in *Liber Faceti.*

> "Quando Deo servis utrumque genu sibi flecte;
> Ast homini solum reliquum teneas sibi recte."

p. 88. *The adder.* "The nedder," as the text puts it quaintly, in the old, correct form. The serpent in *Genesis.*

p. 88. *Mysloset.* Apparently from the root *lose;* hence, to lose amiss, *i.e.*, to lead astray; but the form appears to be passive, not active. Perhaps the idea is that the serpent himself was *lost* for his wickedness; but this seems far-fetched.

p. 89. *Solace . . . makes.* One of the many traces of Scotch. The original rhyme must have been *mas.*

p. 90. *St. Ambrose.* Archbishop of Milan, 340–97. He wrote an ethical treatise *De Officiis Ministrorum*, in imitation of Cicero's *De Officiis;* but whether or not this injunction is found therein, it occurs in almost the same words in *Liber Faceti:*—

> "Si videas aliquem casurum siue cadentem,
> Non ride: sed ei te prebe compatientem."

p. 90. *More and less.* If *at* means *that*, the sense is, that everybody understands it; but the context seems to call for the meaning: that you yourself do not fully understand.

p. 91. *Opens his lip.* Text:—

> "Lest men say to gossip or couth (friend),
> Yonder is a man without mouth."

p. 91. *To staunch,* &c. So in *Liber Faceti:*

> "Si videas fratres inter se bella gerentes,
> Neutri confer opem; sed eorum corrige mentes."

p. 92. *Three oxen,* &c. Another proverbial voicing of "Two's company, three's none."

p. 93. *Red man, i.e.,* red-haired. Presumably this distrust of red-haired people as treacherous was based on the old tradition that Judas was red-haired.

p. 93. *His courtesy,* &c. The meaning is: he must needs be discourteous who stirs fingers and toes, &c.

p. 96. *Stocks with him.* Doubtless, because the castle gate would be the most conspicuous place of punishment.

p. 96. *What he will deem.* What judgment he will pronounce by law.

p. 96. *Wesselle clothes.* The meaning is not clear. Dr. Furnivall suggests *vessel-cloths;* but the phrase is still doubtful unless it alludes to ecclesiastical coverings, which, however, would not be in the porter's keeping, and which would certainly not be sold. Possibly, *wassail-clothes, i.e.,* garments kept perhaps for occasions of special revelry; or, it may be, the sense is that the porter must keep a look-out that vessels *and* clothes, in general, be not stolen and sold by servants or others.

p. 96. *Sits with him,* &c., *i.e.,* he chooses his own companions.

p. 97. *Four pence apiece.* Dr. Furnivall found statutes against excessive prices, but no stipulation of the sum mentioned. Perhaps it was the fixed price in the author's shire. It is cheap enough, only four shillings, at the outside.

p. 97. *Cupboard.* Probably that in which the canopies and curtains were stored when not in use.

p. 98. *Liveries.* Not uniforms, but *deliveries, i.e.,* of rations, or, as in this case, fuel for their own rooms.

p. 98. *Holly keen, i.e.,* it filled the fireplace like an arbour from Good Friday until All Hallows Day.

p. 99. *On his yard score, i.e.,* make notes by a sort of tally on the wood.

p. 99. *Six pence,* about five shillings to-day. According to Russell, four ordinary persons made up a "mess."

p. 99. *The cause he has it in score, i.e.,* if the cook quarrels about the expense, or the panter wants extra bread (reward) brought on. In cases of dispute, the steward was referred to.

p. 100. *Shall harbour, i.e.,* the marshal has charge of all other officers, except the usher in the chamber. John Russell combined the two functions.

p. 100. *Gentleman, yeoman-usher, i.e.,* two, of different social standing.

p. 100. *Make litter.* The making of a pallet-bed I understand as follows. The mattress is nine feet by seven, made of loose straw, for the most part; but with a sort of framework on all four sides, made of bundles (wisps) of straw to keep the sides firm and the great mass of straw in its place; and the whole is to be kept level. Text: *On legh unsunken,* which seems to mean, not in hills and dales.

p. 101. *As a man by the neck, i.e.,* the button was put into a loop resembling a noose. The end of the line is not clear. Perhaps (1) the man hangs light as the flesh drops from his bones on the gallows; (2) the button hangs light because it has no body; (3) the adjective was dragged in for the rhyme.

p. 102. *Boards, trestles,* &c. For the chamber only, as I understand it, the hall having its own groom.

p. 104. *In strong stead* (text, *styd*) *on pallet he lay.* The line is certainly corrupt, and I can make no sense of it. From the context I gather that *lay* is the present optative of the verb meaning to place, not the past tense of *lie. He* seems to refer to the servant, as in the next line, and not to the master who is already "winking." In that case *In* (Sc., *ane ?*) *strong stead* must represent something that he places on the pallet—what, I do not know.

p. 105. *Many are false.* So often in the romances of the time.

p. 105. *Wax so green.* Seemingly the steward's accounts were kept first on tablets, and afterwards copied into books.

p. 106. *Surveyor.* His duty was to examine the dishes and see that everything was right before it went to the table.

p. 112. *Duke John's house.* As his father was king, the man referred to must be John of Gaunt, Duke of Lancaster, who died 1399.

p. 112. [*Wide*]. The passage seems corrupt. The text says:—

> "The selvage to the lord's side within,
> And down shall hang that other may win."

p. 118. *Starven. Starved* is still used, dialectically, to mean, nearly dying of cold.

p. 119. *Will eat.* Russell, in his directions to the carver, specifies choice bits, as the wings (first left, then right) of capon or hen; the legs of quail, lark or pigeon; of fawn, kid, lamb, first the kidney, then the rib; shoulder, then rib of pork, sides of rabbit or hare, &c.

p. 119. *Lief and dear.* This seems to mean only that he might, if he liked, keep a choice bit for a stranger.

SYMON'S LESSON OF WISDOM FOR ALL MANNER CHILDREN

MS. Bodley 832, fol. 174, about 1500. It seems to be unique, and of the author or copyist I know nothing.

p. 123. *Wall.* The passage suggests Lydgate's poem, giving an account of his school-days, especially :—

> "Ran into gardens, apples there I stole,
>   To gather fruits spared hedge nor wall,
>   To pluck grapes in other men's vines
>   Was more ready than for to say matins."

p. 124. *Schate.* The context seems to demand the meaning fence; but the nearest to the form given here seems to be the Scotch *skathie.*

p. 125. *When he is passed.* The allusion seems to be to a middle-class boy in a cathedral school, who, as a chorister perhaps, would be familiar with the bishop's presence, to whom therefore the reference would be pertinent and vivid.

HUGH RHODES'S BOOK OF NURTURE

The Boke of Nurture, or School of Good Manners for Men, Servants, and Children, with Stans Puer Ad Mensam, newly corrected, being necessary for all youth and children. The British Museum contains three early editions, of 1550 [?], 1568, and 1577; and Dr. Furnivall mentions two others as printed between 1551 and 1586.

There is considerable difference between the editions of 1550 [?] and 1568, and that of 1577. H. Jackson, the printer, or some unknown editor either worked from a very imperfect copy or wilfully altered the meaning in many cases; and further, broke up the long rhyming couplets of the original into stanzas of four short lines, the second and fourth rhyming. Naturally, the first and third contain the greatest number of changes. I have used the oldest edition, only modernising the spelling, herein departing from Dr. Furnivall, who printed from that of 1577.

The Book of Nurture, which forms the main body of the work, is preceded by *The Duties of Parents and Masters*, *The Manner of Serving a Knight, Squire, or Gentleman*, and *How to Order your Master's Chamber at Night to Bedward*, all in prose, and is followed by a poem *For the Waiting Servant*, which I have omitted as more adapted to grown serving-men than to children, and by various rules and maxims.

From the colophon we learn that the author was Hugh Rhodes of the King's Chapel, who early in the poem declares himself "born and bred in Devonshire," as his language showed. However, I can discover no traces of dialect.

Nothing further is known of him. The probabilities are that he was Master of the chapel children, whose duty it was to direct their singing, and generally look after them and order their behaviour; but his name does not seem to appear on any royal household list, as far as I have observed.

p. 127. *Briefs and longs*. Expressed in musical terms, perhaps because Rhodes was a music-master.

p. 128. *You . . . thee . . . thy.* These pronouns seem throughout to be used indiscriminately, referring to the same antecedent, and so I have retained them.

p. 135. *Phantasy.* Here *taste, inclination.* Obsolete. See N. E. D., *Fantasy* 7.

p. 136. *Stick.* Probably toothpick. Erasmus wrote of them twenty years before. Cf. *Introduction*, p. xxvii. But indeed we read in Old English of a "tooth-spear."

p. 138. *Checkmate.* Perhaps the meaning is: done for, as far as manners are concerned. But later editions read *Jack-mate*, of which the sense seems to be: that, you think yourself as good as he, *i.e.*, your action shows too great familiarity.

FRANCIS SEAGER'S SCHOOL OF VIRTUE

The title continues: *and Book of Good Nurture for Children and Youth to Learn their Duty by. Newly perused, corrected and augmented by the first Auctor, F.S. With a brief declaration of the duty of each degree.* Anno 1557, &c.

This indicates plainly that there had been an earlier edition. Seager was a poet and translator who flourished 1549–63. He seems to have come of a Devonshire family, and was perhaps the Francis Nicholson, *alias* Seager, who was made free of the Stationers' Company in 1557. Among other things, he translated from Alain Chartier, and also made a rendering of the Psalms. His *School of Virtue* shows as little originality as poetic merit, but it seems to have been popular in his day and long after, as it was revised by Robert Crowley and extended by Richard Weste during the seventeenth century.

RICHARD WESTE'S SCHOOL OF VIRTUE

This was printed in 1619, and about fifty years later was added to an edition of Seager, revised and extended by Robert Crowley; hence, the sub-title, "the Second Part." Weste's treatise is believed to be unique. Of its contents, Dr. Furnivall published only *Demeanour in Serving at the Table*, from Bensley's reprint, 1817.

p. 161. *Gellius.* Flourished in the second century A.D., and wrote the famous commonplace book, *Noctes Atticæ.*

p. 163. *Serve God*, &c., alludes perhaps to serving at table.

p. 164. *Glumly.* Text: *glouting.*

p. 164. *Hedgehogs' right, i.e.,* be not bristling with frowns.

p. 164. *Nor imitate with Socrates.* From this it would seem that Socrates, like Vergil, was roughly handled in the Middle Ages.

p. 165. *Stork . . . elephant.* The idea seems to be : don't make outlandish noises.

p. 166. *Like an image pictured*, &c. Sixteenth-century pictures of the winds are commonly so drawn.

p. 167. *The lips set close*, &c. The idea seems to be merely that pouting lips are not mannerly.

p. 168. *Clitipho.* A comic character in *Heautontimoroumenos.*

ease remember that this is a library book,
and that it belongs only temporarily to each
person who uses it. Be considerate. Do
not write in this, or any, library book.

DATE DUE

AP 01 '92			
FEB 22 '95			
MAY 2 0 1999			
NO 8 04			
11/27/09			
GAYLORD			PRINTED IN U.S.A.